The Essential
SOCIAL MEDIA
MARKETING
HANDBOOK

The Essential
SOCIAL MEDIA
MARKETING
HANDBOOK

A New Roadmap for Maximizing
Your Brand, Influence, and Credibility

GAIL Z. MARTIN

CAREER
PRESS

Wayne N.J.

THE ESSENTIAL SOCIAL MEDIA MARKETING HANDBOOK
Edited by Roger Sheety
Typeset by Kara Kumpel
Cover design by Jeff Piasky
Icon images by Rachael Arnott/shutterstock
Printed in the U.S.A.

To order this title, please call toll-free 1-800-CAREER-1 (NJ and Canada: 201-848-0310) to order using VISA or MasterCard, or for further information on books from Career Press.

The Career Press, Inc.
12 Parish Drive
Wayne, NJ 07470
www.careerpress.com

Library of Congress Cataloging-in-Publication Data

CIP Data Available Upon Request.

For Larry, Kyrie, Chandler, and Cody.
Writers' families have infinite patience.

ACKNOWLEDGMENTS

Thank you to the crew at Career Press including Michael Pye, Laurie Pye, Lauren Manoy, Adam Schwartz, and all the others who brought this book to life. Thanks also to my agent, John Willig, and to the wonderful, knowledgeable experts who agreed to be interviewed and quoted in this book. I'm always grateful to my family for all of their encouragement and support. Finally, thank you, readers, for joining me on this adventure through the ever-changing landscape of social media.

CONTENTS

Section Four: Beyond the Basics

— Section One —

Setting the Course

Chapter One

Virtual and Reality: How Social Media Changed the World

Without social media, today's world would be a very different place.

Smartphones, 4G bandwidth, widespread public Wi-Fi, and adoption of social media across all age groups have made a whole new, instantaneous level of communication and connection possible with game-changing results. Social media showed us a new realm of possibilities, and in exchange, we've changed in what we want, need, and expect from social media.

Why should you care? Social media's impact on the world changed the business environment forever, presenting unparalleled opportunities and permanently shifting customer expectations. It's no longer a question of "whether" you need to use social media in business; if you expect to remain profitable, what you really need to know is "how" to keep up with the changes in social media strategy and use these dynamic, constantly evolving platforms to maximize your brand, influence, and credibility.

Let's start out by taking a look at some of the key ways social media altered the world in which we do business, because you'll need to understand the shifts so you can take full advantage of the strategies you'll learn as we move forward.

Immediacy

Forget postcards, letters, and e-mail. Forget the six o'clock news, the morning newspaper, or this month's magazine. Social media enables us to live in the "now." We are "in the moment" more than ever, in ways never before possible. We see what a friend across the country or across the world is having for dinner a moment after the plate arrives on the table. We watch streaming video from a cell phone user in another country and we see what that person sees in real time.

Not too terribly long ago, phone calls were the only immediate form of communication. Live video feeds required expensive, complex equipment and the resources of a major TV news channel, along with crews of trained personnel.

Now, whether it's the Arab Spring, the tsunami in Sri Lanka, or an altercation at a traffic stop anywhere in the country, someone will post video, maybe even a live stream. We see history and tragedy as they unfold in real time without the buffer of news anchors or TV networks editing or censoring. We go online to find breaking news instead of turning on the TV. Even in our personal lives, we check out someone's Facebook page to see how they are doing, where they're going on their vacation, or what they did today.

We have grown accustomed to living our lives played out for the world to see on a scale beyond what even the celebrities of yesteryear could have imagined. Not only are we used to the immediacy of sharing our lives moment-by-moment and getting instantaneous feedback, but it's easy to become addicted to the rush of validation that comments, shares, likes, and retweets provide. We are all stars of our very own reality show.

Use the immediacy of the Internet and social media to your advantage by inviting your audience at live events to post video, live-tweet, or upload photos to Facebook. Recognize that via social media, you can engage with people who could not attend your event in person, but who can participate virtually by responding to the in-the-moment content you and other attendees post as the event unfolds. Take advantage of the immediacy inherent in video by making use of the ever-expanding range of apps that make Web video easy. You're limited only by your imagination.

DISINTERMEDIATION AND DECENTRALIZED INFORMATION FLOW

All hail the rise of the citizen journalist. Gone are the days when the network news teams of the broadcast TV channels curated the information, images, and opinions that reached the public. Social media, the Internet, and cell phones have made everyone a reporter, commentator, and broadcaster.

On one hand, this new decentralized information flow and its lack of institutional filters, censors, and controls frees us to digest information raw. We can find a nearly endless amount of information on every topic, posted by all kinds of sources. To the extent that this makes it much more difficult to suppress information or carry out disinformation campaigns, disintermediation is a good effect of social media.

No wealthy individual, no powerful government, no feared criminal is powerful enough to gag the Internet. WikiLeaks, Edward Snowden, and many other whistleblowers and informants have proven time and again that secrets will come out. And when a media hoax is perpetrated or an urban legend goes viral, it falls as quickly as it rose to prominence, exposed by bloggers, fact-checkers, and sites like Snopes.com.

On the other hand, not all news sources are created equal. Although some may strive to be unbiased or to at least honestly admit their bias, many others take a "caveat emptor" approach. "Astroturf" organizations—groups with earnestly populist sounding names that are actually funded by political or business organizations with a definite agenda—can be difficult for the average reader to quickly identify. We can now report and retrieve our own news, but we must also authenticate the information provided to us by others.

Social media has also changed the concept of "expert." Subject matter experts can reach niche audiences easier than ever before, without the need for travel or speaking engagements. Blogs, videos, Webinars, and social media share a subject matter expert's insights and connect directly with the intended recipients.

At the same time, it's now up to the individual to determine whose expertise is authentic. Although experts have proliferated on social media, validating expertise has become a thorny proposition. Before social media, the experts who gained fame held some kind of hierarchical power. They worked for a large corporation, for the government, or for a nonprofit or religious organization, which functioned as a level of vetting. Expertise was also determined by earned degrees, such as MD, PhD, etc., or professional membership, which served as an endorsement from the organizations granting the degrees or accepting qualifications for membership.

Social media makes it possible for people with subject matter knowledge, computer skills, and an engaging personality to reach millions without needing to obtain the approval of gatekeepers. This opens tremendous possibilities for knowledgeable people with an entrepreneurial spirit, and has built the fame and fortune of many Internet gurus. Yet it can also be difficult to vet Internet experts because their information and platform is often entirely self-reported and their validation relies on anecdotal evidence and testimonials.

What does this mean for you? Social media presents you with a golden opportunity to establish yourself as an expert in your field of expertise and to reach the world with your information. Establish your credibility and build your brand through the valuable insights you share on social media, and use the connections you make to expand your influence.

CROWDSOURCING

We've always relied on the opinions of our family, friends, and neighbors. Yet it has never before been as easy to tap the "hive mind" of hundreds or thousands of acquaintances for information, opinions, and funding. Social media changed how we research, validate, and interpret information, and thanks to sites like Kickstarter, IndiGoGo, and GoFundMe, it has democratized the concept of "angel investing" on a massive scale.

Wikipedia and other wiki-powered sites amass the collective knowledge of individuals on every topic imaginable. Not only is the scale of that collection different from anything that came before, but so is the fact that no powerful body of experts serve as gatekeepers and moderators. We now have the essence of popular knowledge at our fingertips, but at the price of having that information tainted by our commonly held misinformation.

Once upon a time, not so very long ago, commentators and opinion leaders held sway because they were noted experts or at least installed in their positions by organizations with cultural legitimacy. Rank-and-file opinions were relegated to the Letters to the Editor column. Now, that paradigm has been flipped, and the rise of sites like the *Huffington Post* amplifies the voices of anyone and everyone with insights to share.

Likewise, we used to turn to expert-written guides to inform our purchases, such as Consumer Reports, Zagats, Frommers, AAA, or the *New York Times'* best-seller list. Now, we make purchasing decisions based on the consumer feedback on Angie's List, Yelp, Amazon, and similar sites. Social media has completely changed how we seek out and consume information or weigh input on decisions great and small.

The takeaway for you lies in realizing potential customers may put far more stock into the ratings and testimonials provided by other clients than in fancy industry awards or accolades from traditional media. Customer service is more transparent than ever before, so you'll want to make sure that satisfaction is part of your ongoing strategy, and that you encourage happy clients to rate your services and provide quotable feedback.

CONNECTEDNESS: GLOBAL VILLAGE AND MARKETPLACE

Thanks to social media and the Internet, we can have one foot in the tangible, local world, and the other in the virtual, global village. Our friendships are no longer constrained by proximity or the expense of old long-distance communication methods. We are free to find individuals and groups that share our interests, concerns, passions, and viewpoints regardless of physical location. Or we can strengthen bonds with far-flung friends and family without depending on the annual holiday card, newsletter, or hit-or-miss phone calls.

We form friendships and business relationships with people we interact with on social media that are every bit as real as those forged through in-person interaction. Our need for connection has not changed, but we have expanded the perimeter of our village and marketplace. The consequences are significant. Thanks to social media, every company, no matter its size, has a greater potential advertising reach than huge firms could even dream about in the days when traditional media reigned supreme.

Networking is also now unchained from physical proximity, meaning that you can easily develop customer, vendor, and resource relationships with people all around the world. When your social media engagement funnels prospects and customers to a well-functioning online sales site, you've got a recipe for success. Using social media to remain connected and engaged with prospects and customers between sales can yield more referrals and decrease attrition. Existing customers who understand the full scope of your offerings and are updated on new and expanded products and services are likely to buy more frequently.

Though social media can help you expand your opportunities in the global marketplace, be aware that it also exposes you to worldwide competition. Customers are no longer limited by proximity, and although that creates benefits for you, it also benefits your competition. To stay on top of the market, you may need to up your game and embrace new technology, like video, or expand your strategies for building connection and engagement. Social media platforms and tools change swiftly, which requires willingness on your part to be constantly learning and adapting.

PRIVACY AND SECURITY

Love it or hate it, social media changed how we think about privacy and security. Facebook, Tumblr, Instagram, and Periscope make it easy to share our thoughts, reactions, itineraries, locations, and purchases on a nearly moment-by-moment basis. On one hand, that creates the immediacy and engagement that enables our friends and followers to feel like they are riding shotgun on our lives. Yet that intimacy comes at the cost of privacy, and details made public cannot be taken back.

Thanks to data mining, "cookies" that track online browsing and purchases, our Google histories and the information we share on social media, advertisers and social media sites can gather a frighteningly in-depth profile of our interests, consumer habits, opinions, and personal data. A few decades ago, people complained about the junk mail in their mailbox or spam e-mails. Those now seem like crude, fumbling attempts at advertising compared with pop-up ads on Amazon or Facebook that reflect your latest searches or purchases. As a consumer, the loss of privacy is unsettling. As a potential advertiser, the specificity with which an audience can be targeted using social media bodes well for effective positioning and successful campaigns.

Privacy is the conundrum of the social media era. Drawing the line between "sharing" and "oversharing" has personal and professional ramifications. Posting a Facebook rant on a bad day or firing off a tweet in anger can lose you clients and tarnish your reputation. Post a photo or a comment without context and you might invite a firestorm. Yet pull back too much, build the walls too high to defend your private life, and your social media lacks authenticity and personality.

Before Facebook and social media, only celebrities needed to worry about their public "persona." Simple professionalism worked just fine for everyone else who went about their business largely out of the public eye. Social media has given us all much more than the "fifteen minutes of fame" artist Andy Warhol predicted awaited everyone in the future. Now that each of us has the ability to broadcast globally in a medium that never sleeps, having a personal PR survival strategy is essential.

Realize that when you show the world your "professional" side, you are presenting a carefully curated version of the real you. Ideally, you will find the balance of revealing enough personality, appropriate humor, warmth, and emotion to attract people to you as a person while still retaining boundaries around the parts of your personal life that you want to keep off-limits to the general public.

This is where the security aspect comes into play. Many experts who share a great deal about themselves on social media draw the line at sharing information about their children or family members for safety reasons. Using apps that tag your location can be great when promoting your appearance at a business event, but less desirable when it comes to exposing your every move during your private time. This is especially true for people who have experienced real-life or online stalkers or Internet trolls and who have reason to fear for their physical safety. Even without such threats, common sense suggests that it's not wise to post about upcoming trips or vacations that leave your house unoccupied or to broadcast your hotel information or itinerary if traveling alone. Make sure you know what information your social media apps are disclosing about you and how to turn those options on and off to protect your privacy and security.

Put your best professional foot forward on social media and remember that, unlike Vegas, what happens on Facebook never stays on Facebook.

LANGUAGE AND PARADIGMS

Before social media, trolls lived under bridges, birds tweeted, and friends were people we knew personally. Thanks to Facebook, Twitter, and other sites, our language has evolved to reflect our online lives. The dictionary now recognizes new words like "livestream," "hashtag," and "selfie" and has added to the definitions of older words like "troll" and "tweet."

Part of using social media successfully and being part of the online world requires you to learn and use terms appropriately. I've heard people misuse or mangle social media terms and though they indicated that they thought it was funny to do so, unfortunately it made them seem outdated and behind the times. Social media is here to stay, and it is a valuable and intrinsic part of building your brand and maximizing your influence. You build your own credibility when you make the effort to keep up-to-date on the language of social media and use it correctly.

Social media has not only altered language, but also our paradigms. Concepts like crowdsourcing information and crowdfunding projects didn't exist before social media made them possible. Likewise, the dark side of social media reframed our understanding of aggression with highly publicized cyber-bullying incidents and situations like GamerGate, which showed the power of social media stalkers and Internet trolls to cost people their reputation, livelihood, personal safety, and in extreme cases, their lives.

Because social media dramatically increases an individual's reach, it's especially important to think before you tweet or post, especially if you have accumulated a large audience of friends and followers online. Although that reach enables you to help others by connecting them to your mission and services, a single hastily posted message in a moment of anger can do a great deal of damage to someone's reputation or livelihood.

BLURRING VIRTUAL AND REALITY

Social media is rapidly evolving, changing from a completely text-based medium in its early days to increasingly embrace—and favor—photos, audio, and especially video. As more of our senses are engaged, our connectedness grows. As consumers, we have progressively moved more and more of our lives online. We shop on Amazon, consult with a business mentor via Skype, log into a secure page to e-mail our doctor with a question, check a mobile app to request a book from the library, and see if our prescription is ready at the pharmacy. Nearly every business and organization with which we interact in the real world has a social media presence (and possibly an app) to provide additional on-demand content, help, and connection.

The line between "real" life and "virtual" reality blurs every day. As devices like Oculus Rift and other virtual reality (VR) systems are perfected, we will see VR spill over into social media as well. Remember what a breakthrough it was when real estate agents could post 360-degree videos online? Now imagine that enhanced with VR technology that makes everything the customer sees feel like it's live and in 3-D. Think of the possibilities for product demonstrations, live events, personal coaching, and site tours when it becomes possible to share and provide an immersive experience that feels real via social media.

As 3-D printers improve their abilities, consider a future where a link on social media could transmit the information necessary for a prospect to download and print a sample of your product—much in the same way that someone can share an e-book today. As the boundaries blur between the tangible world and the online world, expect to see new ways to deliver goods and services via social media, and think ahead to what opportunities, challenges, and threats that raises for your business.

We don't know exactly what the future holds for social media, but given its track record, expect continual change and innovation that rewards individuals and organizations that remain agile.

THE LAST WORD

Social media has changed the world, and in turn, the world has changed what it demands from social media sites. Businesses of all sizes and types are scrambling to determine how to make the most of this new and rapidly evolving technology. Finding the best ways to integrate social media into your planning is imperative. Sitting out the digital revolution is not an option for businesses that want to thrive.

NEXT STEPS

1. Make a list of all the ways your business currently uses social media.

2. As you read this book, jot down ideas and names of sites that might be of use. Take 10 minutes a day to browse new social media sites that look useful, and get familiar with how they work.

3. Sort your ideas by the target audience you want to reach, and make notes on whether the new sites you're discovering increase your branding, credibility, influence, or a combination of all three.

Chapter Two

Creating a Social Media Plan and Platform

In order to be successful on social media, you'll need both a plan and a platform.

Your plan is your strategy, laying out a roadmap that helps you determine what you want to say and to whom, what you hope to get out of building relationships, how you are going to measure success, and what actions you intend to take to achieve your goals.

Your platform is the foundation from which you build your online credibility. Your platform establishes and reinforces your expertise. It's the cumulative impact of all of your content and social media interactions, which support (or diminish) your brand and extend (or negate) your influence.

Ideally—and with careful thought and preparation—your plan and platform work together in harmony, supporting and strengthening each other, constantly adapting and changing to meet shifts in consumer taste and technological advances.

Which comes first, the plan or the platform? Usually, it's a little of both, evolving together. Because your platform comes from the ways in which you share your subject matter expertise, many people are well along in building their platform before it occurs to them to create a social media plan to extend and share it. For someone just starting out, creating the plan and platform simultaneously will likely keep you from heading down dead ends or wasting time going off on tangents. Starting with the plan means assessing what expertise you want to use for your platform, as it's unlikely that you're going to decide to suddenly become an expert overnight. On the other hand, it's very common for people not to realize how special, rare, and sought-after their knowledge or skills are when they spring from native talent, abilities the person has always just taken for granted was as simple for everyone else (but isn't).

MAKING IT HAPPEN

What do you want from social media? If you're like most people, you've got several results in mind. The most common might include:

- Gather prospective customers (your tribe).

- Engage current customers and prospects.

- Raise your visibility as an expert.

- Draw the attention of media and influencers.

- Get people to sign up for your newsletter, seminars, events, or downloads.

- Demonstrate your influence by growing the number of people who like and follow your pages.

All of these are valid expectations from your social media investment. In fact, many people will seek to achieve several if not most of these goals through the course of time. But as you begin your social media plan, I suggest that you prioritize your goals because it is easier to add a goal once others have been achieved than it is to pursue several objectives all at once.

Let's look at what's involved with each of the six goals and see how they influence the direction of your social media plan and how you use your expert platform. We'll get into the "how" details later.

Gather Your Tribe

We'll cover this topic in depth in Chapter Three, but for now, I want to talk about the key strategic elements involved in this goal. Gathering like-minded people who are good potential clients, referral sources, collaborative partners, and resources requires content that establishes your expertise and also attracts readers to you not only as an expert, but as a person they like, know, and trust.

No matter the topic, there are plenty of experts. You want to attract the people who will be the best fit for you because something in your background, approach, or personality resonates deeply with them beyond just your knowledge. Out of all the experts in the world, you want them to pick you because you are most in sync with them.

Merely sharing information—no matter how brilliant—won't do it. You have to be willing to share that information in your own unique way, and that means revealing your personality. Don't be afraid. You don't have to overshare. In fact, what you do choose to share on social media should be carefully curated—but not artificial, and not distant.

Confused? Don't be. Think about the comfortable, casual feel of a business retreat where people remain professional and yet lose the stuffy formality of the office. In those settings, people smile more, joke around a little, have fun, and maybe even do things that are mildly silly, all in the name of teambuilding and developing relationships. That's exactly the kind of atmosphere you want to cultivate with your social media: relaxed, business casual, personable, and fun. None of that compromises your expertise. But those elements make you approachable, and they open the door for people to get to know you better and trust you because they like you.

Engage Current Customers and Prospects

Think of all the ways you currently stay connected with your current and former clients as well as interested prospects. Perhaps you send out an e-mail newsletter or hold live educational seminars or open house receptions. Maybe you support a golf tournament or a charitable event or host a retreat or large event. All of those efforts are focused on strengthening your relationship with these valuable people and remaining on their radar in between purchases so that they will buy from you in the future and refer you to others.

Social media gives you the chance to achieve the same goal. In fact, social media works very well to enhance and augment all of those real-life activities by bringing another layer of immediacy and reinforcement to the situation. But social media is unique in that it allows you to strengthen those bonds every day without requiring you or your customers and prospects to leave the comfort of their desk chairs.

Don't make the mistake of thinking that social media is merely a broadcast platform, like your own personal newspaper or radio station. That's why the word "social" is in the term "social media." Being social requires two-way interaction. That means you want to start a conversation and participate in conversations that others start. So part of building engagement means actually interacting with people, not just pushing out content.

Engaging is easy. Ask open-ended questions on your Twitter page and Facebook page, and then respond when people answer. Don't argue— converse. Nurture back-and-forth discussions like in an in-person conversation, and create a safe space on your page for people to feel heard and respected. Moderate comments and block trolls or argumentative people. Reflect genuine interest in the opinions of the people who follow you. And when you see interesting content in your news feed posted by someone else, show your interest by liking, sharing, and commenting. That opens new conversations—and you never know where they'll go!

Posting video, like with Facebook Live, allows the viewer to see and hear you and provides a greater sense of connection than a purely word-based post. Mix things up with photo memes and quotes. Throw in some travel photos of your own, photos of your dog or cat, and pictures you snap of something interesting in your day. All these things make you feel more approachable, more "real." People who might be a little intimidated by your expertise may feel safe reacting to a cat picture you've posted, and that can be enough to break the ice.

We'll talk more about techniques to create engagement in future chapters, but for now, keep the concept in the back of your mind, and think about the kind of conversation-starters you might be able to use on your social media platforms.

Raise Your Visibility as an Expert

Social media is an essential part of creating your expert platform. You'll want to help your friends and followers recognize the nature and scope of your expertise without beating them over the head with it. Fortunately, there are easy, fun ways to accomplish your goal.

Establishing expertise has two components: knowledge and fame. To be an "expert" you need to be highly knowledgeable in your niche. Your credibility increases if you can prove that you are "famous" for your expertise.

You demonstrate knowledge when you post a link on your Facebook page or Twitter feed to a blog you've recently written that showcases your expertise. The same is true for a video or audio where you share content, a photo meme with a handy tip, or a helpful answer to a question. Whenever you participate in a discussion in a group on Facebook or LinkedIn and provide good information, you demonstrate your expertise.

Likewise, when you share useful links to content by other experts, you not only demonstrate expertise, but you also begin to create a web of reciprocity with other influencers. Sharing a link to an article, blog post, or video that you know will be of interest to your audience shows that you get out into the real world and that you aren't just on social media to blow your own horn. You demonstrate that you sincerely care about helping your followers get the very best information available, even if that means tapping into the knowledge of others. Of course, you win points for recognizing valuable content and you look confident and secure when you're willing to acknowledge and respect the expertise of others.

You demonstrate your "fame" when you post links to articles you've written or been mentioned in by well-known authors or news sources. Likewise, posts about your own books, videos showing you on stage giving a presentation, and links to events where you'll be speaking all underscore that others acknowledge your expertise and that you are known among influencers as being good at what you do. This reassures people who may just be getting to know you, confirming your credibility. It taps into our social bias that looks for group validation.

Fame (which is always a relative statement) in this case means outside acknowledgment by a news source, fellow expert, publisher, organization, and so on. When you share links that show other people recognizing you as an expert, they help to build your credibility. Now you're not the only one attesting that you know your topic and have value to share; other people who have already proven themselves and who may be well-known to your audience are validating you.

Draw the Attention of Media and Influencers

Getting noticed by bloggers, news sites, event planners, and other experts is a key part of building your expert platform, and creating circumstances that increase the likelihood of that discovery should be part of your social media plan.

Several things happen whenever you are mentioned in the media or by other influential people. First, the fact that you are considered to be worthy of note and your content important enough to be shared provides social validation to your expert status. Now it's not just you claiming to be an expert; other people are calling you an expert, so it must be true. Second, your reach and fame increase every time you are mentioned by someone else. The more people who read your content, the more potential customers you make a connection with. And the more often people hear your name, the greater the likelihood that they will remember you as an expert in your field. Name recognition is valuable. It's the "I've heard of her/him" that makes someone pick up your book in a store, read one of your articles, or consider you as a resource. It's also valuable to be a known name when you approach potential collaboration partners, pitch a story to the media, or apply to speak for an event or organization.

Obscurity is your greatest enemy as you build your expert platform. Yes, everyone starts out as a "nobody" and gradually earns their way to expert status. But social media's vast reach and the opportunity for valuable content to "go viral" can shave years off the time it takes to get to become a household name, at least in your field or niche.

When you post a link to an article or interview that features you as an expert, other people in the media take notice. Reporters and bloggers follow trends and are always looking for the "next big thing." When one site taps your expertise, others don't want to be left out. Visibility begets more visibility. Not only that, but by virtue of the fact that a news site deemed you worthy to interview, other sites see your expertise as being validated and therefore making you safe to use as a source for their own site. You've gotten past a gatekeeper, and others now recognize you as legitimate.

Likewise, what you say in one article or interview might spark a reporter's interest for a follow-up question, or the opportunity to explore a related tangent. The topic of a speech might lead a blogger to ask you for a tied-in blog post or interview. You can utilize this tactic to pitch articles, speeches, and guest blog posts to the media and event organizers, creating a web of related content that all underscores and strengthens your area of expertise. When you share the links to those articles and events on your social media, it reinforces your platform.

Influencers are people whose opinions hold sway with other important people. They may or may not be experts in their own right, but they are always well connected and highly regarded. It's easiest to identify experts as influencers because of their fame. Yet people without personal name-recognition can be very influential. Most bloggers and reporters are not personally well-known, but they determine whether or not you are interviewed or asked for an article on sites that magnify your reach. Few event organizers are famous, but they choose who will speak on stage in front of hundreds or thousands of people. Editors and publishers are usually unknown outside their industry, yet they decide whether or not to publish your book.

You can connect with influencers on social media in several ways, and your plan should lay out a road map for how you'll make this happen. LinkedIn is a great way to make these connections, and we'll talk more about that in depth later. One great way to get on an influencer's radar in a favorable way is by sharing links to their content on Facebook and Twitter, making good (and non-self-promotional) comments on their posts, and offering to be a resource if you can help them make a connection that would be valuable for them. Give first, and build a like-know-trust relationship.

Realize that influencers might well be among the people who like, read, or follow your social media. They may be sizing you up to see if you are legitimate, or assessing your professionalism. Maybe they want to watch quietly for a while before approaching you, or perhaps they're keeping you in mind for when the time is right. That's why it's so important that you carefully curate your social media presence to always put your best foot forward and be on your best professional behavior. You never know who might be watching!

Get Sign-ups

Your plan should address how you are going to increase your e-mail list and encourage people to like and follow your social media pages. It's important to have permission from your audience to be in touch. A prospect might find you by accident, but once you've been discovered, you don't want to leave your ongoing relationship up to chance.

Although e-mail newsletters might seem passé, they have an important advantage in that you own your permission-based mailing list. On the other hand, the likes and follows for your social media sites, however important, can vanish in an instant if the site suddenly goes away.

All of your social media pages, as well as your blog and Website, should have a clear, easy-to-find way for people to join your newsletter and discover your presence on Facebook, Twitter, and other sites. You can encourage sign-ups by offering free content, providing admission to an invitation-only event, holding drawings for one of your books or products, or requiring people to enter their e-mail address in order to get something they want, like an e-book or download sample. Your plan should allow for switching up the incentives to keep your offers fresh and new.

Demonstrate Your Influence

The size of your social media following is another indicator of fame. Rightly or wrongly, people will judge your legitimacy as an expert in part by how many people recognize your expertise by following you in some way. Human nature assumes that the more popular you are, the more you deserve popularity. It's the classic bandwagon fallacy, but it's still true. So although you don't own the contact information for your social media followers, it's still important to attract them to your pages and give them an incentive to like or follow you. Not only will they be more likely to see your information, but their aggregate presence will also help to assure the world that you are legitimate.

A second level to this idea of fame-by-association lies in looking at who your friends are and their importance. Does that sound too much like high school? Unfortunately, not much changes. You're still judged on the company you keep. Someone checking you out might look first at how many friends or followers you have. A savvy social media user will then look to see whether your friends reflect your expert status. If none of your friends or followers are other professionals of the same or higher status as yourself, you lose credibility. After all, if you're a true expert, you must know other experts and they should value your information.

The next step up comes from not only being friends with influencers and other experts, but by having them actively comment and like your content. This requires effort on their part, and shows ongoing engagement and a level of endorsement. Your mom was right: you are known by the company you keep. When your social media reflects ongoing conversations with other experts and influencers, your credibility rises.

Another level of validation comes when other experts and influencers actively share your content on their sites. When your quotes, books, events, posts, and articles are being reposted by well-known people, you gain additional legitimacy because they found your content valuable enough and trustworthy enough to share with their own tribe. They would not endanger their own credibility by sharing questionable information, so this reflects a further level of vetting.

And of course, when you share the content of other experts on your own sites, you are doing the same for them, helping them expand their reach and influence. Social media rewards and incentivizes authentic reciprocity.

If you don't have a gazillion friends and followers yet, don't despair. It takes time to build a following, unless you start out as a celebrity. It's much better to build your following organically and steadily than to get involved with any shady deals to "buy" followers to bulk up your numbers. Sure, you could amass 40,000 followers overnight, but it only looks impressive until someone takes a look at your following and sees that they're from overseas hotbeds of Internet scams. Not only will you lose credibility, but the list you "amass" by dubious methods will do nothing for your sales. Because they aren't really interested in your subject, they'll never buy from you, forward your content, or become a real resource. You're much better off with a smaller following of people who are sincerely into what you have to say and are good potential clients. Don't get caught up too much in the numbers. Provide good content and encourage engagement and your following will grow.

THE LAST WORD

Social media shouldn't be left to chance. To accomplish your goals and use your time wisely, you need to have a strategic plan based in a solid understanding of the strengths and weaknesses of the various sites and how social media works. As with anything of value, it takes time, effort, and patience to build your following, but you'll see progress day by day.

NEXT STEPS

1. Identify your ideal audience and make a strategic social media plan to map out how to find and gather prospective customers (your tribe).

2. Develop useful and interesting content to engage current customers and prospects.

3. Plan your time and make being present on social media a daily task. Be consistently visible on social media to raise your visibility as an expert.

4. Retweet, share, like, and comment on good content by other experts. Follow social media feeds of bloggers, reviewers, and influencers. Learn from what they do.

5. Create incentives to get people to sign up for your newsletter, seminars, events, or downloads.

6. Engage your tribe with conversation, questions, and good content to grow the number of people who like and follow your pages.

CHAPTER THREE

BUILDING CREDIBILITY AND GATHERING YOUR TRIBE

Before people buy from you, they need to like, know, and trust you. Social media is an unparalleled way to reach individuals around the world in ways to get known, demonstrate your likeability, and earn their trust. Successfully doing that doesn't happen by accident. Your social media plan needs to include strategies and actions designed to gather your tribe and build your credibility. Doing that requires effort and consistency, but the cost is minimal and the payoff is potentially huge.

SECRETS OF TRIBAL SOCIAL MEDIA

As I mentioned in the previous chapter, social media isn't broadcast media; it's intended to be a two-way conversation. Your prospects and customers want more than your expertise and your skills: they want to get to know you. You don't have to bare your soul or overshare, but you need to learn the trick of being personable without being too personal.

Being personable online is a bit of an art, and it requires mindfulness because it's very easy to come off as distant, programmed, and impersonal online. Today's customers are media savvy, and they are wary of experts who seem too perfectly packaged, as if every sound bite is pre-planned. They're looking for authenticity and transparency, and they want to make a personal connection—that's what leads to the like-know-trust cycle.

Being personable on social media means bridging the gap between the podium and the audience, coming down off the stage to have a real, unscripted conversation. Realize that your conversations on social media can be intentional and purposeful without being scripted. You can still circle around your key points and reinforce your message, but do it in a way that doesn't sound rehearsed and canned.

Social media is a natural platform for extroverts who never get too much face-time with an audience. Yet it can also make an introvert into an online rock star, because when you're interacting with people on social media, you aren't looking out on a sea of faces in a live audience. You're safe behind your computer screen, in the privacy of your home or office, which can be comforting for those who don't feed off the energy of a crowd. Just remember that nothing you say on social media is ever off the record, nor does anything posted ever truly go away.

Think about the last in-person networking event you attended. Remember how you worked the room, introduced yourself to new contacts, and started conversations with people seated at your table. Use the same interpersonal skills on social media, and you'll go a long way toward gathering your tribe. Ask questions that draw people out and get them to talk about their needs, concerns, and desires. Be a good listener. Don't lead with a sales pitch or be too quick to ask for the business. Give first, whether it's a tip, a referral, or a recommendation of a resource. Relax and be your best self so others begin to get to know you and find common ground.

You do all these things naturally at a live event if you've been in the business world successfully for any length of time; now you just need to get comfortable acting the same way on social media. And just like at a luncheon or conference, you have probably developed some questions that help you quickly determine whether or not someone you're talking with is a good potential customer. Shift your social media conversation in the direction of your qualifying questions, so that you continue to engage with people who are truly interested and weed out the tire-kickers.

People have been gathering as tribes around campfires since the dawn of time. Think of your social media pages as campfires that draw people who are attracted to your topic, expertise, and unique personality. You want to find the campfires (sites) where your tribe is already gathering and gradually invite and incentivize them to follow you home to your campfire. One way to do that is by becoming active with blogs, Facebook groups, LinkedIn groups, and industry sites that resonate with the people you want to serve.

Don't make the mistake of joining sites and immediately starting to sell. That is a huge turn-off, looks unprofessional, and might get you banned from the site. Give first. Join with the intent to be a helpful resource. Answer questions, suggest service providers, and share useful content like links to articles and blog posts. Demonstrate your expertise and generosity. Let people experience your credibility. Help them to like, know, and trust you. When they're ready, they'll follow you back to your page or send you a message wanting to connect.

THE POWER OF STORIES

One of the best ways to engage with your tribe is by sharing stories. People are hardwired to listen to stories. We tell stories to impart our most essential information. From the time you were born, you have been listening to stories that tell you who you are, such as family stories about ancestors or past events, and heritage stories about your ethnic and religious background. We tell stories to explain life and death, and we weave narratives to explain and contextualize everything that happens to us. Stories have power.

What are your stories? They are an essential part of differentiating yourself from competitors because they define you and they shape your unique approach to the services and expertise you provide. No one else has arrived at this point in time by exactly the same road you have traveled, but your ideal tribe will be drawn to similarities between your journey, your approach, and their own. Demonstrate that through your stories, and your tribe will find you.

One concern I hear from a lot of clients is the fear that they don't have any exciting stories to tell. When I drill down, I've never found this to be the case. It's much more common to discover that clients are so used to the amazing results they get with their clients that they dismiss the significance of the outcomes or take the successes in stride as if achieving them was no big deal.

Nothing could be further from the truth. This is not the time for humility. For your clients, the outcomes you achieve may have saved the day. They may seem nothing short of miraculous. Don't make the mistake of thinking that "anyone" could have created those results. You brought your unique perspective, honed from your personal journey, to the situation and that's what enabled you to approach the problem in that particular way.

Don't take your miracles for granted. They make the most powerful stories.

I learned this secret when I was running the communications department for a major rehabilitation center. We specialized in working with people who had experienced a spinal cord injury, stroke, or traumatic brain injury. It was my job to tell the hospital's story, and I knew we did amazing work—miraculous work. I would see patients be wheeled in on stretchers, on body boards, and I would hear about the horrific car accidents or factory accidents that caused the damage, broken backs, broken necks, skull fractures, or I would see elderly patients wheeled in looking so frail and unable to do anything for themselves.

And in a few months, I would see many of those same patients walk back out on their own, go back to work, to raising families, to playing the sports they loved. I knew we had stories to tell.

But when I went to talk to the therapists, they told me they didn't have any stories because they couldn't think of anything unusual. The miraculous had become commonplace, so they didn't even think it was special anymore.

So what are your miracles? Do you help people get out of the kind of debt that made them think they would never be financially sound again? Do you help people buy the home of their dreams, a home they never thought they'd be able to afford? Maybe you're a light worker. Do you help people find inner peace and transformation when they are held back by their past mistakes? Or maybe you're a health professional, helping people live happier, healthier, longer lives by making changes to their diet, exercise, and habits. Have you ever thought that what you do is miraculous? It is to the people whose lives you've changed.

Are you taking miracles for granted and missing out on the amazing, heart-centered stories that could bring a flood of new clients to your business? Clients who desperately need what you do, who are looking for someone with your skills, but who won't realize that you're the one who can help them until you tell a story that lets them put themselves in the picture.

Miracles are precious. Don't ever take your miracles for granted.

Testimonials, case studies, before-and-after photos, and videos are all types of stories. The best stories don't just share the result; they also describe the journey, including set-backs, obstacles, and mistakes. You may think that owning up to set-backs would decrease your appearance of expertise, but in reality, it boosts your credibility by showing your transparency and willingness to back up and start over. When you show a little bit of vulnerability, it helps others relate to you, because perfect people are intimidating. Realize that anyone can solve an easy problem, but it takes a real seasoned professional to know how to overcome obstacles.

Testimonials, case studies, and stories have important similarities and differences. All of them focus on results, but they get to the outcome in different ways, and they each have a different function.

Testimonials tend to be short. They involve a named customer attesting to a successful outcome. A testimonial usually tells nothing of the process, and it may not provide specifics about the nature of the result except to confirm that the customer's needs and expectations were met or exceeded. Testimonials are a type of crowdsourced information, providing validation of expertise and credibility and giving a prospect confidence to engage your services based on the number of satisfied customers.

Always ask customers to give a testimonial when you finish up a successful engagement. Many people forget to ask or feel uncomfortable bringing up the subject and by doing so, lose out on good recommendations. If you've done good work and achieved your customer's goals, don't be embarrassed about asking for an endorsement. Consider it another type of payment for a job well done, because testimonials have significant value. Not only do prospects consider the number of testimonials, they also look at the degree of enthusiasm and the types of clients providing the recommendations. Customers want to feel comfortable trusting you, and knowing that others have worked with you successfully builds that trust.

The second mistake many experts make is not guiding a client to give a useful recommendation. Think about the difference between "Joe did a really good job" and "Joe helped me increase my ROI by 30 percent in six months." Both are positive, but one is much stronger than the other. What makes a strong recommendation? Move past generic superlatives like "great," "awesome," and so on. Although those words are nice to hear, they are meaningless without details to back them up. Encourage your clients to make note of something quantifiable, like a sales or ROI percentage increase, or a dollar figure of increased sales or savings. Having specifics lets the reader judge for himself whether or not your performance was "awesome."

How do you guide a customer to give the kind of recommendation you want? Many experienced business people have provided testimonials before, so the idea of having a desired format may not strike them as unusual. Some might even ask you to draft a couple of possible testimonials and let them tweak the wording themselves. Or you can provide a template to get them moving in the right direction.

When you ask for the testimonial, let the client know that you want their comment to be as useful as possible for prospects, and that you've discovered most people want to know three things: 1) What problem you were hired to fix; 2) Whether or not you were easy to work with; and 3) What outcome you achieved, preferably with some kind of measurement, percentage, or dollar figure. Truth be told, most customers will be grateful for the template, because if they're not already pros at testimonials, they'll be glad for a model so they can "do it right."

You can share testimonials on social media in several ways. You might want to get your clients on video talking enthusiastically about your services. Perhaps you catch attendees right after one of your events and record the video while they are still caught up in the excitement. Ask a client to post their testimonial on your Facebook and LinkedIn pages in addition to supplying you with their quote. Make sure they include their photo with the testimonial on Facebook and on your Website, because that underscores the fact that this is a real person endorsing you.

If you're in a business that has tangible, visible results, here's where a picture can be worth a thousand words. Always make sure you snap a "before" picture and an "after" shot. Combine those before/after photos with your customer's testimonial and post it on Facebook, Pinterest, Instagram, or Tumblr. Words are persuasive, but nothing seals the deal like seeing the results for yourself.

Case studies are longer than testimonials. Realize that here I'm talking about marketing case studies, not academic or medical cases, which have an entirely different set of rules. A marketing case study should be no longer than two pages. Like any good essay, it should have a beginning, middle, and an end. Case studies benefit from details, so share as many facts and figures as your client will allow. (Any case study that includes the customer's name or the name of their business, or which shares identifying details must be approved by the customer.)

In a case study, you have more leeway to describe the nature of the problem, the process by which the problem was solved, and the result. Case studies are often posted on your Website, where they function to illustrate in more detail how you work with your clients and the kind of approach you take to solve problems. Case studies shouldn't sound academic, but they generally have the feel of an essay or business article, retaining an element of detachment. They are a step up from testimonials, but though valuable, they still don't share the most powerful information.

You can also share your case studies in business articles that you write or in a blog post. Don't forget to include before/after pictures, if applicable, for extra punch. If you write a blog post or have your article published in an online magazine, be sure to post the link to Facebook, LinkedIn, and Twitter for maximum impact.

Stories are the most powerful tool in your marketing arsenal. They go beyond case studies by including more emotional impact. A good story makes it clear to the reader what is at stake, and the consequences of failure. It lays out what has to be accomplished, and heightens the drama by detailing the setbacks or obstacles that threatened to derail the project. Finally, a good story also satisfies the reader by explaining not just the factual details of the final success, but also what success means emotionally for the client.

In fact, a success story works much the same as a good adventure. Good stories engage the reader, create a level of emotional involvement between the reader and the characters in the story so that the reader cares what happens, and provides an emotional payoff where the reader feels the protagonist's success for himself. To do that, your story requires five key pieces: a hero, a dragon, a damsel in distress, a few plot twists, and a happily ever after ending.

You are the hero of the story. Your customer is the damsel in distress, and whatever the problem is that you've been hired to solve is the dragon. The plot twists are the setbacks and obstacles you meet along the way, which prove your expertise and underscore your credibility. The end result and the emotional payoff constitute the happily ever after ending. This is your five-part recipe for a successful case study—and it works.

I shared this recipe with a client who came to me for help with their case studies. They just didn't know how to talk about their accomplishments and make it interesting. Because of that, they were losing out on contracts, and they needed to land more business. So I asked them to tell me what happened. My client said, "We get hired to take over projects that aren't working and fix them. It saves the client time and money."

Well, that's nice, but it's not exciting. So I asked him to tell me about one of their recent projects, and he did, but in that same kind of very dry, matter-of-fact, bare bones way.

But I heard a blockbuster movie.

So here's how I heard the story:

They were IT consultants, and a really big bank had hired them to take over a multimillion dollar project. This project was going to have a big impact on the bank's bottom line. Millions of dollars and thousands of jobs were riding on this project.

And the project was late. In fact, the project was not just late, it was overbudget—a lot. Even worse, some of the key people on the project had quit. But that's not all. The people who quit had very rare skills. So rare that there were only a hundred people in the whole United States who could do what they did…and now those valuable members of the project team were gone. The project was sinking fast. So when the consultants came in, they had a big task. But that's where it was good that they were different from other consulting firms.

In a lot of consulting firms, once you leave the firm, you're dead to them. They drop you from the holiday card list. But not this group. They stayed in touch with everyone who had ever worked for them. They gave them good references, sent them holiday cards, and considered them alumni.

So when my client needed help to save this project, they put out the word to all their employees—and to their alumni. They sent out an SOS to find people with those very rare skills, skills that were almost impossible to find.

And guess what? Two of their alumni just happened to have those skills. And yes, they were willing to come back and tackle the project.

Because their firm was different, because they treated their former employees like alumni instead of traitors, they got the project back on track. They got it back on budget. And they got it done on time.

That's an adventure!

My client's company was the hero. The bank was the damsel in distress. The project was the dragon. The hard-to-find skill was the plot twist. And for anyone who has ever been afraid of not making a project deadline, coming in on time and on budget was the best happily ever after ending you could ask for.

CREATING AND SHARING "RESULTS ENVY"

Your goal here is to create what I call "results envy." Results envy occurs when the customer reading the story identifies with the problem, pain, and fear of the client; recognizes their own situation in the plot twists; and wants the successful outcome on both an intellectual and an emotional level. Results envy is powerful because it spurs action. A good story has the reader thinking: "I need that." It validates your abilities in the reader's head while connecting deeply with the heart as well. That's a very powerful combination, and one which makes it very easy for a prospect to become a client.

When you're telling your story, get the reader's emotions involved. Detailing the problem, pain, and fear are essential for a compelling story, because they let the reader know what is at stake. The problem is the symptom, and is often the issue you're hired to fix. Ramifications of the problem create the pain, which gets worse the longer the problem continues. The fear is what your client is afraid will happen if the problem can't be solved or the pain gets out of control. So for example, a computer crash might be the problem your firm is hired to fix. The pain would be the lack of ability for the client's company to provide services, communicate internally or externally, accept orders, pay employees, or collect payments. The fear lies in what happens if the pain continues: cash flow difficulties, lost sales, inability to make payroll, loss of customers to competitors, and even bankruptcy. The prospects who read your stories will identify with the pain-problem-fear and see themselves in the case study. They'll recognize the risk and stress from their own situation, and they'll feel the relief when a solution saves the day. Then they're very likely to connect with you to see if they can get some of those heroic results for themselves.

The testimonials, case studies, and stories that you share on social media need to create results envy for a reason in addition to being the hook that draws your prospects closer. Results envy also helps you overcome the ego/budget factor.

First of all, I want you to realize that you don't sell services. You don't sell products. You sell solutions to problems. If you're a consultant, you help people accomplish what they can't figure out on their own. If you sell a product, you provide a tool to people to do something they can't do without your tool.

And that's the problem. Your customer has to admit to being a failure before they are willing to buy your product or services.

See, most people won't buy a solution to their problem until they have tried to fix it themselves. Either they don't want to spend the money (budget) or they don't want to admit they can't do it alone (ego). Think about the last time something broke at your house. Whether it was a clogged drain or a glitched garage door, I bet you tried at least once—maybe more—to fix it yourself before you called in a professional or went out to the local hardware store to buy a replacement.

Why? Because you didn't want to spend the money, and you figured "it can't be that hard." By the way, plumbers love this kind of thinking, because it usually means by the time they get the call, the problem is 10 times worse than it started out. But the truth is, we try to fix it ourselves. We duct tape things together for as long as we can. We work around the broken part until we can't stand it anymore, or until it doesn't work at all, or until someone else refuses to put up with it and makes us do something about it.

We have to fail before we're ready to buy—and we have to admit to ourselves that we have failed. We don't like that. In fact, we'll try really hard not to come to that conclusion. That's why people put off buying your products and services.

They're not ready to fail. They're not ready to admit that they can't do it themselves if they try a little harder or a little longer. They're not ready to put away the duct tape and admit it's really broken.

Case studies—stories—make it easier for them to get past the ego/budget factor by showing them what happened to someone else. Someone who had a problem just like theirs. Someone just like them. Someone with the same fears and hopes, who was in a lot of trouble, like them, until they saw the light. Someone who trusted you and your product or service to help, and then got the jackpot, got the Holy Grail, got the solution and peace of mind and money and good night's sleep and no more acid reflux solution. When they get to that point in the story, they've got results envy and they want what you've got more than they want their pride and more than they want their money. Now you've got a customer.

Another important reason to share stories that create results envy is to validate the return on investment. For 99 percent of us, money is finite. There isn't enough to do everything, so it's a constant series of trade-offs. If I buy this, I can't buy that. Invest here? If so, can't invest there. There's always an opportunity cost, something you miss out on because you did something else and you can't do both.

If you want a customer to spend money with you, that's money they can't spend on something else. Not only do you have to get them past that ego/sticker-price issue, you also have to get them to want what you've got to offer more than what they're passing up to get it.

How do you do that? With results envy.

When your prospect wants the outcome so much that he or she can taste it, touch it, smell it, feel it, and imagine themselves living with the solution to their problem, he will validate the ROI to himself. You won't have to do it. Your prospect will argue themselves into the purchase. She'll talk herself out of her objections, because she is already sold on the outcome. Results envy will make the ROI argument for you.

How do you share results envy stories on social media? One of the best ways is to incorporate the story in a live presentation and then post a link to the video of your speech on Facebook, LinkedIn, or Twitter. Or, go right to the viewer and record yourself telling the story on Facebook Live or in a video you upload to YouTube. Use the story (complete with photos if possible) as a blog post or article, and be sure to share the links on your social media sites. Tell the story with a series of photos and to-the-point captions on Instagram. Results envy stories work well on social media because they grab readers emotionally, and because they are also a natural conversation opener, which leads to comments, likes, and shares.

Your ideal tribe will be attracted to the stories you tell, the way you tell them, and the insights you draw, and that's an advantage that is uniquely yours.

CREDIBILITY AND CHARISMATIC INTEGRITY

Credibility and what I call "charismatic integrity" are essential for maximizing your brand and influence on social media and for attracting and growing your tribe. They are essential to your platform and are the make-or-break difference for your success as an expert.

Credibility is more than believability. Believability has to do with the factual nature of the information. Credibility has to do with whether or not you trust the source or the bearer of the information.

The Internet makes fact-checking easier than ever before. Yet if factual information is shared by an untrustworthy source, doubt remains. Streetwise consumers know that the best lies are those built on a grain of truth, and they will be wary if they do not feel confident that the source or messenger is reliable.

Likewise, the phrase "don't shoot the messenger" reminds us that telling a truth that is difficult or painful to hear can result in the listener shutting down or fighting against the bearer of harsh facts. There is an art to telling the truth in such a way that the listener is receptive, especially when dealing with sensitive subjects or information that requires the recipient to make a significant shift in their worldview or self-image.

Integrity goes beyond credibility. Credibility has to do with the reliability of the source conveying information. Integrity is the long-term pattern of behavior demonstrated by the source that proves not only truthfulness, but honesty, loyalty, reliability, and other positive traits. Charisma is the aura of attractiveness and charm that draws others to a person. An untruthful person can be highly charismatic; in fact, this is how con men operate. But a truthful, credible person of high integrity without charisma may appear stiff, pious, self-righteous, or condescending.

Some lucky people are born with high charisma. For everyone else, it's a relief to realize that charisma can be learned. And the simple truth is that tactful honesty, tempered with sincere concern for someone else's well-being, lies at the heart of real charisma.

Be present and be real. Showing sincere interest and giving someone your complete attention makes you highly charismatic to the person to whom you're speaking, whether that's an individual or an audience. Make eye contact. Let your passion for your subject shine through. In your social media, let your followers glimpse the other subjects or hobbies that you're passionate about outside of your work. Share photos and short videos, provide insights into your hobbies or trips, talk a little about what you do for fun.

Your just-for-fun posts help to demonstrate your charisma, but so do your videos and Facebook Live posts where you let people see your personality and your humor.

Charisma tends to describe the in-person attraction people feel to you, but that appeal can carry over into your writing as well. Remember that online comments don't get tempered by body language or the tone of your voice, so you can be easily misunderstood unless you make sure your message is clear. Avoid sarcasm, as it does not translate well to the written word. Always be yourself, unless you're not a nice person—in which case, be your best self.

THE LAST WORD

Storytelling is an art, but it can be learned. Too many marketing stories lack emotional connection, fail to generate results envy, and don't speak to the problem-pain-fear element. When you speak to your ideal audience (tribe) with a compelling story, sales happen.

THE NEXT STEPS

1. Think about the clients for whom you've achieved great outcomes. Make a list of potential stories you could tell.

2. Sort your list of stories to see which ones might be good case studies and which would be better done in the hero-damsel-dragon-plot twist-happy ending format for a bigger emotional impact. Be sure to identify the results envy!

3. Keep the budget/ego challenge in mind as you create your stories. Make the outcome from your services or product too good to pass up.

4. As you think about satisfied clients, also make a list of people who would be ideal for testimonials. Approach them with a plan in mind.

AN INTERVIEW WITH MICHAEL PORT

Michael Port is the *New York Times/Wall Street Journal* best-selling author of *Book Yourself Solid* and *Steal the Show*. He is also a top speaker and coach whose work emphasizes integrity and accountability. Here, I talk with Michael about "charismatic integrity" and related topics.

Q: What's the relationship between charisma and integrity?

A: Charisma and integrity don't necessarily show up together. People can have one or the other, or both. On the Internet, you can say anything you want to about yourself, and the Internet may or may not support it. A person's online brand identity might not match his/her offline identity.

In my industry—books, speeches, training—I get comments like "I want to thank you for your integrity." I don't think you should get a pat on the back for integrity like it's rare; it shouldn't be a surprise to encounter it, but people don't often experience it.

People say, "Oh my god, you're just like I thought you'd be." I'm disappointed that it's a surprise for them. People have had bad experiences with others.

I like social media because it's so public, which increases accountability. Your personal brand identity can be a positive constraint. Having a constraint isn't necessarily negative. When your brand is about something you stand for and you use social media to spread the message, you stand for the message and not just the tactics, and that keeps you accountable.

Go back to how you want to be known in the world. Use social media as a positive constraint to remain in line with the way you want to behave in the world. The more intentional you are in the world, the harder you work to stay accountable.

I believe that the level of success we achieve has a connection to the level of responsibility we can handle. If you get stuck, work on being able to handle more responsibility and things tend to open up. A company with one full-time person and a part-time assistant is very different from running a major company.

Using social media helps keep me in line with how I want to be in the world. I stay away from political issues and conflict and scathing reviews. What we do online tells the world who we are. Be deliberate with what we share online. Be conscious and intentional. Position yourself intentionally online and offline.

Q: What have you learned about building engagement on social media?

A: The two most popular posts I've ever had on Facebook were personal. One was when my grandmother turned 103 and the other was when I shaved my head. Why would someone care? It's fascinating to me that I can write a post with information that is going to change your business, but I won't get the same response as when I share how I see the world.

Customers knowing we have skills is a baseline. They choose you because of an emotional connection. If you don't focus on making an emotional connection, you'll have a hard time competing on services alone.

We focus on the culture of our online and offline communities. We design offerings so customers interact and build a sense of community. We create rules to lead to the kind of community we want to have, and we want our customers to feel like the community belongs to them.

People comment on the results they've gotten and on our community. We have a big focus on bringing our community offline as well.

I'm part of a tight Facebook group for speakers. I'm on the group daily. My wife and I set up the first offline Meetup for members. People came from all over the world. Moving offline as well as online builds trust.

Q: Your background includes training and work as an actor. Not everyone has that benefit, and we're not all extroverts or born with high charisma. Can performance and charisma be learned?

A: Many performers are not extroverted. They need time alone or with family to recharge. You can be gregarious, but be an introvert. If you like people and learning about what people think and do, it helps you connect better than just entertaining people.

If someone was shy as a young person, they may hold back with others, but if you are curious and read people well, you can do better than a gregarious person without empathy.

Find ways to leverage your personality and gifts to serve who you are.

Presence can be learned from a performance perspective. Presence reflects preparation, confidence in who you are, being relaxed because you're prepared. If I don't create great content and rehearse and sculpt stories, I can still bomb regardless of charisma.

You develop presence through the development of craft. You can become a great presenter even if you're not a natural entertainer.

— Section Two —

Building a Foundation

CHAPTER FOUR

THE MIGHTY THREE: FACEBOOK, TWITTER, AND LINKEDIN

Dozens of social media sites exist, but it always comes down to three: Facebook, Twitter, and LinkedIn. Love them or hate them, they are the three main sites (along with YouTube, which we'll talk about later) and they have a large and diverse following. When my clients complain that they are overwhelmed with their social media choices, I tell them to start with these three because they're where the action is.

Facebook, Twitter, and LinkedIn may be three of the most popular social media sites, but they are very different from each other. Think of Facebook as a party where everyone goes to see and be seen, meet new people, and have fun. The atmosphere is casual and laid-back, and people may get caught up in conversations from time to time with people they don't know.

Twitter is more of a cocktail party, where the emphasis is on short, witty conversations and working the room, connecting briefly with many people, but keeping it personal.

LinkedIn is like a business networking event. Everyone's professional, a little more buttoned-down, and on their best behavior. You'll meet new people, but it's easier and more comfortable with a personal introduction. Conversation remains mostly business-oriented.

Facebook, Twitter, and LinkedIn are different, but don't let that scare you because each site is a tool to accomplish a similar goal through varying styles of conversation and engagement. Just as you learn to adapt to the different group norms of the offline organizations in which you're a member, navigating these sites and their differing cultures will soon become second nature.

FACEBOOK: WHERE THE WORLD GOES TO MINGLE

Facebook is loud and noisy and wonderful. It's the crossroads gathering place for planet Earth. Facebook is meant to be a conversation, not a broadcast, so you want to look for ways to attract and engage your current clients and best prospects in a way that leverages your credibility and reinforces your brand.

Don't worry; it's easier than you think. Several years ago, when I wrote *30 Days to Social Media Success*, the most common question I got when I spoke to groups was, "I'm on Facebook: now what?" Many business people truly did not know what to say when they had to sit down at the keyboard. Fortunately, I think we've gotten past that point, so that now business owners are looking for ways to maximize their brand and enhance their reach while underscoring their expert platform. We've come a long way in a short time!

Having a casual conversation on Facebook is easy. Striking up a two-way discussion that engages your tribe and either gets them talking about their wants and needs or imparts helpful information in an unstuffy way takes a bit more thought. One way to provide valuable information and broaden your connections at the same time is to share posts from other people's pages that you find useful or think would be of interest to your tribe. You can also share links to articles in online magazines and news sites, as well as to your own blog posts. Build goodwill and make new friends by liking and commenting on interesting posts on the other people's newsfeeds. Always be polite and avoid confrontation or controversy.

Get creative and mix things up by sharing photos, videos, and text. Visual memes of inspiring quotations are very popular, and easy to make. When you make a photo meme, use a picture you either have taken yourself or for which you've purchased the rights. Attribute the quote, and make sure you have your own Twitter symbol at the bottom so people who like the meme can find you. Respect copyright by sharing the link to a photo or article; never save someone else's material to your computer and upload it. If you put out an e-mail newsletter, realize that many newsletter software programs enable users to automatically send links to their Facebook and other social media sites whenever a new edition is sent out. This is a great way to broaden the readership of your newsletter, give non-subscribers a free peek, and encourage new sign-ups.

Not surprisingly, Facebook has evolved quite a bit since it made its debut. Not only does it have close to two billion users, but it has shifted many aspects of the user experience with corporate advertisers in mind. In the early days of Facebook, no one thought of the site as being of interest to business users. It began as a platform just for college students, and gradually expanded to be open to everyone. Small business owners and entrepreneurs were among the first to see Facebook's marketing and networking potential, and in an effort to segregate personal and business conversations, Facebook introduced its "fan pages" as an alternative to the more personal profiles.

For a while, that worked. Business users invested time and effort (and eventually money) in building their following on their Facebook page. Facebook created the ability to pay for targeted advertisements, and then to "boost" posts on business pages. Business users got used to sharing content, confident that a majority of their followers would see what they posted. But through the years, users have noticed that the organic reach (the people who see a post without a boost or an ad) has steadily declined to be only a small percentage of the number of people who have "liked" the page.

Facebook is cagy about its strategy, but those in the know suspect that the decline in organic reach comes from an algorithm designed to encourage more paid ads and boosts. Likewise, users who pay for boosted posts have reported a decrease in the reach of posts through time for the same level of ad spending, creating diminishing returns. I've seen this happen on my own boosted posts, where the number of people estimated to be reached for a $20 boost to the identical target audience has decreased by thousands from one year to the next. It's a profitable advertising revenue strategy for Facebook, but something business users need to recognize and learn to work around.

Video is experiencing a similar transition in the way Facebook treats various online video sources. Facebook is highly territorial in its stance toward other social media sites it considers to be competitors, like YouTube. It appears that the Facebook algorithm favors "native" video (uploaded via Facebook Live or from a user's hard drive) and suppresses the reach of videos uploaded from Google Hangouts, YouTube, and similar sites. That's something to keep in mind when you're trying to reach as large an audience as possible with your content on a shoestring budget.

Facebook can be aggravating, and its frequent changes to its algorithms and rules are vexing, but it's still the biggest game in town, and you are absent at your own peril. Many prospective clients will check out your Website first and then both your Facebook business page and your personal page, if it's publicly accessible, to get a sense of who you are and whether or not they want to work with you. Make sure you always put your best foot forward!

TWITTER: SHORT AND SWEET

Twitter confounds a lot of people. It's a micro-blogging site that limits your post to 140 characters, or about one long sentence. That's not too different from most conversational replies, so I'm amused to find so many folks struggling with what to say.

Twitter is great for sharing quotes, one-liners, and observations about trends, topics, and news events. It's perfect for sharing a link to an interesting article, cool photo, or your latest blog post or video. Ask a question, and get your followers involved in a conversation. Share a survey or poll link, and discuss the results with your tribe. You can live tweet when you travel or attend a presentation, sharing the highlights of what a speaker says or interesting landmarks you see. When you're speaking, have an assistant or someone in the audience live tweet your best comments. Or, give your assistant good one-liners from your speech in advance and pre-schedule the tweets to run while you're speaking. Tweet the Amazon link to your latest book, or to a good book you've just read. Share a link to your newsletter, or give a signal boost to a colleague who has tweeted something interesting. The possibilities are endless, limited only by your imagination.

The news feed on Twitter moves much faster than the wall on Facebook. So although posting more than one or two times a day on Facebook might annoy your online friends, you can post about once an hour on Twitter without wearing out your welcome. As with all your social media platforms, vary what you post. Try to post 5–10 times about something not sales-related before you post a link to something you're trying to sell. Note: content-rich articles, videos, and blog posts that you've written don't count as "sales-related" if the information is helpful and it's not the wind-up to selling something.

The law of reciprocity thrives on social media. Sharing quality content by people you admire helps your tribe and establishes you as a giver, winning points with both your audience and the people whose content you are forwarding. Your sources, in turn, will be likely to return the favor by forwarding helpful content that you have created to their tribes, increasing your visibility and extending your credibility.

Realize that when you retweet content by someone less well-known than you are, you are giving someone a hand up, and when someone more famous than you are retweets your content, they have done you a solid. Even sharing content between two people of equal status is a win, because your tribes are unlikely to completely overlap. When you share valuable content that is not all self-generated, you gain influence because others see you as confident and generous. You also demonstrate that you are well-connected to information and to other experts, and your followers begin to rely on you to vet the most valuable content and serve it up on your newsfeed, enhancing your value to them. When you share your own content along with the other information, its credibility is heightened.

Using hashtags (#) are another way to enhance the visibility of your posts. Hashtags denote words or phrases that are popular, so when you incorporate a hashtag in your tweet, you assure that your tweet will show up with other tweets that include the same tag. So if you tweet "Send your loved one a card for #Thanksgiving," your tweet will show up when any-one searches on #Thanksgiving or grouped with similarly tagged tweets for #Thanksgiving under the Trending column. Likewise, you can watch the Trending column for popular hashtags and use those that relate to your content to raise visibility.

Using hashtags can gain your tweets visibility when the tagged word is trending in popularity. But be careful not to bait and switch—readers take a dim view of thinking they're getting a post on one subject only to find content that has no connection to the tag. In other words, don't tag your posts with the names of famous celebrities if it's not relevant to your topic!

When you share content mentioning someone else, be sure to use their Twitter "handle," which is the name they use on Twitter with @ in front. So on Twitter, my nonfiction handle is @GailMartinPR. Why should you use it if you retweet me or mention me? That way, I see your post in my feed. I can thank you, return the favor, and retweet you. We all win! Don't begin a tweet with the @ symbol, or only people who follow both of us will be able to see the tweet. You'll unnecessarily limit your reach. Likewise, don't tag people (especially famous people) who have no inter-est or connection to the subject of your tweet. It's the Twitter equivalent of name-dropping, or worse, bragging about being besties with a celebrity you've never met. It's okay to tag a famous expert if you have a legitimate reason to think there is interest or mutual benefit, but don't do it often.

Because you only have 140 characters, save space when you tweet a link by using a shortened URL. Use a site like *www.bit.ly* to shorten a long Web address into fewer characters. Always give your followers an idea of what a link contains, because no one wants to click through blind-ly. Photos increase engagement and stand out on the rapidly updating newsfeed. Use photos in your tweets whenever possible and credit the source of the image if it doesn't belong to you.

Twitter also lets you create lists of specific Twitter followers to help you better manage your newsfeed. When you create a list, you are group-ing people with similar interests or content together. When you click on that list later, you'll see the latest posts from everyone on that list. It's a great way to get a news digest of information by topic or by group. You can create lists and share them with others, or keep your lists private. It's an honor when other people add you to their lists, because it's a way of making sure they catch all your news.

Twitter has begun offering paid advertising. Much like with Facebook, Twitter ads allow you to choose a target audience for your message, and your ad will show up in the news feed of people who fit your target. The ad will note that it is "promoted." You can promote a tweet, your account (to get more visibility and followers), or a trend (a hashtagged word or phrase).

Twitter also offers analytics to see how well your page is interacting with other users. Your analytics page gives you a snapshot of how many profile visits, mentions, tweet impressions, and new followers you've gotten in a 28-day period, and keeps several months of data visible so you can see how your effectiveness changes with time. Other helpful data includes identifying your most popular tweet (measured by impressions or how many people saw it), your top mention (when someone else mentioned you), and your top follower (the person who follows you and has the most followers themselves).

Think of Twitter as the tickertape for the 21st century, the modern AP newswire where we are all generating the news. If you're still unsure about how you want to use Twitter, go check out the pages of top experts you admire. See which types of posts attract you and which don't. Watch how they engage with followers. Get ideas of what works and what doesn't. See if you can tell which accounts have a PR professional managing them (and not the account owner) and which feel more authentic. Then wade in and try it for yourself!

GETTING THE HANG OF LINKEDIN

LinkedIn is the business epicenter of social media. Although its interface is sometimes clunkier than Facebook and other consumer-oriented sites and it is frequently the last to fully embrace new technology, such as video, LinkedIn makes up for its shortcomings by being the place to go for networking.

Though your profile on Facebook and Twitter are important, your profile on LinkedIn is essential. It's the first stop when people want to check out your credentials. Make sure you have a good, current, professional headshot photo, and fill in your professional resume-keeping the information short, accurate, and results-oriented. Write your summary to be engaging and outcomes-focused, conversational, and not salesy. Fill out your educational background so that you can easily reconnect with former classmates who are now business professionals.

Add the skills you think best represent you. Fill out the sections on your volunteer work and honors, and add other information that doesn't fit elsewhere under the "Interests" section.

When it comes to accepting network requests on LinkedIn, two basic approaches rule. The first approach is to limit your network to only those people whom you actually know. This makes sense from the standpoint that you will only want to ask people who know you to make introductions for you, and you will only want to introduce people whom you actually can vouch for. Your network will be smaller, but you'll have a trusted circle of colleagues.

The second approach is to accept any request that appears to be from a legitimate source. If you go this route, it's perfectly acceptable to ask the requester why he/she wants to connect with you. It's also okay to refuse requests from people who appear to have no reason for interest, who might be a competitor fishing for contacts, or whose profiles demonstrate that they heavily self-promote. You'll have a larger network, but you won't know all of your contacts personally.

Invite people you know to join your network. Your ability to e-mail people you don't know varies by the level of membership you select. LinkedIn also frowns on mass-friending, and complaints can get you in trouble with the site. Start off slow by only adding people you actually know, and build out from there. A great way to get to know others is by reading the content they share and then making helpful, insightful, and non-salesy comments or by sharing that content with a link on your own page.

LinkedIn gives you the ability to share photos, status updates, and articles. Remember that LinkedIn has a business focus, so it's not the place for vacation pictures or funny cat memes. This site loves meaty content, and it's perfect for sharing links to informative blog posts and online articles, both your own and those by other experts that you have found useful.

Once you have begun to build your network, give first. Go out and endorse your colleagues and former coworkers. Give recommendations. This is a great way to warm up old contacts, and often results in reciprocity. It's also okay to connect with people who know you well and ask for strategic recommendations and endorsements. Be sure to thank people who do take the time to write a recommendation, and return the favor.

LinkedIn has plenty of helpful features. You can post a job, look for a job, take an online class, and hire a local freelancer. One good way to meet new people is by starting or joining an interest group. When you join a group, don't go in selling. Be a helpful, knowledgeable, and credible resource. Interact the way you would at a networking event. Give first. It takes time, but as people get to know and respect you, they will find you if they need you. Likewise, when you start a group, focus on providing value, not a sales pitch. Create a place where people get valuable content and connections, update and interact frequently and consistently, and your tribe will grow.

Sales Navigator is LinkedIn's built-in CRM-like tool. It's worth exploring, as are the various levels of membership that come with differing features. Pick the level that's right for you—upgrading is always possible.

LinkedIn also allows paid advertising. You can choose from sponsored content (similar to a Facebook boosted post), which draws additional attention to something you post in your newsfeed. Or, you can create a text ad that will appear in the right sidebar. A benefit of advertising on LinkedIn is that the site delivers a business-minded audience, more so than Facebook where the mix is business and pleasure. LinkedIn is also likely to reach an audience of decision-makers who may not be Facebook users.

THE LAST WORD

Doing business in today's marketplace demands accessibility, and that means that if you want to remain visible and influential, you'll need to be a committed participant on social media. Though you may find other social media sites that lend themselves well to your interests and skills, customers will look for you first on Facebook, Twitter, and LinkedIn. Be present in a strategic and consistent way, and you'll go far toward maximizing your brand, influence, and credibility.

NEXT STEPS

1. If you're not already on Facebook, Twitter, and LinkedIn, sign up for an account and make your profile information complete and compelling.

2. Spend some time looking at the Facebook, Twitter, and LinkedIn pages of people who are leaders in their fields. What kind of content do they share about business and about themselves? How do they engage followers in conversation? Jot notes to yourself on what you might do for content and engagement.

3. Start to connect with people you know on the sites before you think about reaching out to strangers. Gather a following of people with whom you're comfortable, and spend some time getting to know the "neighborhood" before you make any big moves.

AN INTERVIEW WITH ELINOR STUTZ

Elinor Stutz, CEO of Smooth Sale, is the author of *Nice Girls DO Get the Sale, HIRED!* and *The Wish: A 360 Degree Business Development Process to Fuel Sales*. *CEO World Magazine* named Stutz as one of "The brightest sales minds to follow on Twitter," while both *Inside View* and Open View Labs designated her as a Top Sales Influencer. Kred rates Stutz in the Top 1% of Influencers.

Q: You've amassed a large following on LinkedIn and used the site very effectively. What have you learned about making the most of LinkedIn?

A: LinkedIn hands us the research we need on a silver platter. Prior to contacting someone, read their profile, as it showcases their life work and pinpoints what they believe to be most important. Those insights provide the best way to begin a conversation.

I recently moved from California to the East Coast, and all of my connections came with me because of my online activity. I was later named a Top 1% Influencer due to consistent interactions on social media.

When I read an interesting article or receive a relatable tweet on Twitter, I search for the person on LinkedIn to learn more about them. And only then do I message them. In just two steps, we're connected.

As I review LinkedIn profiles, I scan through the person's work history and projects they care about. The idea is to find common interests we might share. An introductory message is then sent that points to those interests.

Highly accomplished people are active on LinkedIn. There is nothing to lose by asking someone of this caliber to connect. If my invitation is ignored, it's the same as not asking. However, by asking, many have accepted my request.

I inter-mix platforms. I blog several times a week and embed one of my YouTube videos in each post. The blog is then shared on the major social media sites. Accordingly, I'm on thousands of lists, and built a large social media following. *CEO World Magazine* named me as One of the Brightest Sales Minds to Follow on Twitter.

Through LinkedIn, I've received fantastic introductions within organizations that would otherwise have been either difficult to come by or would not have happened.

I've developed an enormous network through social media. Because of this, incredible opportunities came about. This is all due to the decision I made to participate, and at a time when others said I would kill my business.

I do things differently. I jokingly blame it on the fact that I'm left handed. I'm constantly learning about social media and embracing new thought.

Review your LinkedIn feed to see what catches your attention. Share the content that both you appreciate and know your audience will, too. Click the tab that says, "See who reviewed your profile." Click on each of those to review their profiles, too. If of interest, send a personalized e-mail to offer an invitation to connect.

A few years ago, Elinor had more than 25 million contacts within her three degrees of connection on LinkedIn. Connections known and not so well known, from around the world, encouraged many others to also ask to connect.

AN INTERVIEW WITH VIVEKA VON ROSEN

Viveka von Rosen is a LinkedIn expert and the author of *LinkedIn Marketing: An Hour a Day.*

Q: You've been active on LinkedIn since the site's early days. What shifts have you seen?

A: LinkedIn started in 2003 in Silicon Valley—mostly as a recruiting and HR tool focused on networking and job seekers. While it's still crucial for job hunters and recruiters, LinkedIn is now embracing its sales, marketing, training, and advertising sides. LinkedIn has invested a lot of talent and resources into acquiring or creating features to improve these facets of the platform.

LinkedIn is developing its social selling power with the Sales Navigator CRM [customer relationship management] platform. With Publisher and Pulse, members can utilize content marketing to build authority, credibility, and visibility. LinkedIn purchased BIZO to build out its advertising suite, and Lynda.com to address its membership's need for online education and training.

LinkedIn seems to be focusing more on the sales professional, small business, entrepreneurs, besides its enterprise-sized corporate clients. I think this focus is enabling its members to embrace content marketing/social selling. It was always possible, but not fully supported by LinkedIn before.

There are some weaknesses to the platform. In their attempts to monetize, they have severely restricted the usability. And even some of the Premium features are out of the average small business user's grasp. And then there are simple fixes, like making it easier to use the Get Introduced button! I think the biggest failing to LinkedIn as a platform is that it is not as intuitive as it could be, meaning it's not used as much as it could be.

As far as the future of LinkedIn, it is most definitely headed toward a revenue model (I mean, Microsoft bought them after all!). I always tell my folks, don't think of it as a paid social media site; think of it as a business tool. Use it to connect and engage with key target market audiences. The paid level is most effective.

One new client pays for LinkedIn's cost for the next 10 years. Everything is moving to a subscription basis.

It's so important to assure that your LinkedIn profile is good because it shows up on Google. It's important to have a credible presence on LinkedIn.

What happens is, people get busy and they let their profiles get outdated. Keep it current, make it good, get good photos.

The social media imperative is transparency, authenticity.

A good profile means you don't start selling right away. As they say, you've got to buy someone a drink first before taking them home. It's all about getting people to like, know, and trust you. Private messages are good for that. Update your content, connect, and use Skype calls to nurture and create a business relationship. Think long term.

Pick your face up from your phone and interact with people.

Nurture relationships. Otherwise, having contacts you don't use is like sitting on a pile of business cards you collected at an event and never did anything with. If there are 999 messages in your in-box, you're leaving money on the table.

Q: Should people accept all legitimate invitations (even from strangers) and have an open network, or only deal with people they actually know and have a closed network?

A: I'm at the limit of how many connections I can have. My virtual assistant prunes my connections. It's a balancing act. If you're too small in terms of connections, you're not visible. If you have too many, it's cumbersome. I tag all my customers on LinkedIn, and I only accept invitations if the invitation is customized. If you try to send out a sales pitch without building a relationship first, it won't work.

People underutilize introductions. Only ask someone to introduce you if you know the person well and if they know the person you want to meet.

You can automate your LinkedIn to an extent, but you need to get on the phone at some point and be personal.

Do a little research on promising prospects. Look at their profiles, social media, and timeline.

The key to LinkedIn is looking credible, being able to find, connect, and record ideal prospects. I reach out to five new people each day. Ask questions, make comments, but don't sell. Share a helpful link or article—it doesn't have to be your content. Be helpful.

Customize your invitations and ask them to connect with Inmail. Have a way to manage the connections with some kind of contact management system.

Do some kind of engagement. Mention people, endorse them, and ask them for a quote. Build the know-like-trust element, and then escalate that to a phone call. Look at your current and past clients and reconnect. Ask them for referrals, endorsements, recommendations. Refresh what they know about you and what you currently do.

Q: LinkedIn has been a little slower to embrace video than other social media platforms. What are your expectations about the future of video on LinkedIn?

A: LinkedIn still doesn't have the infrastructure for live streaming yet. You can use and share YouTube or Vimeo in a link in an update. They open up big, which take up space on the timeline and gets attention. You can also embed video within LinkedIn Publisher, with a transcript. People like the authenticity and transparency of video. If you've got video interviews, product demos, testimonials, a sizzle reel, add it to your profile.

In your video, look credible. Be professional.

Chapter Five

Navigating the Google Empire

Google is the ultimate over-achiever, striving to be everything to everybody. Most of the time, they do a good job. The Google line of products aren't all equally spectacular, but even the so-so offerings have the benefit of being tied in to the Google empire.

Let's start with Google, the search engine. Yes, there's Bing and Yahoo, but Google is the 800-pound gorilla of online search. Sure, specialized programs like BuzzSumo or Boardreader search certain parts of the Web very well, but Google serves up a wealth of accurate results quickly. The downside, of course, is that your searches are being tracked and data mined, which is how eerily accurate customized ads magically appear at the top of your page and in the right-hand bar. You can delete your browsing history, but that just affects your screen, not what Google knows about you. If you can live with that, Google is a mighty fine tool.

Google+ is the Schrödinger's cat of the Internet, simultaneously alive and dead depending on how you look at it. As of the writing of this book, Google+ was still online and predicted to stay that way. Yet it's never really lived up to expectations that it would be the next Facebook, either for personal or business use. It's got some very nice features, not the least of which (like all Google products) is that it can be accessed by a single sign-in on your Google home page. The user interface is clean and eye-catching, and plays up photos and videos well.

It's just…lonely out there. Google+ reminds me of being at a mall on a boring Wednesday afternoon or in an airport terminal in the middle of the night. The structure is great, it has a lot to offer, but there's nobody around. So, perhaps, one backhanded benefit to being on Google+ is the lack of clutter and noise. If you can attract your tribe to follow you, or attract current users, you'll have a better signal-to-noise ratio than on more populated sites. Just don't expect to find a user base that is rapidly expanding.

I suspect that Google will either eventually repurpose Google+ or shut it down, so although it's a nice place to post content you're creating for distribution, I'm not sure it's worth making a time investment to actively grow your audience.

Google Hangouts, the online way to record video via Google, is in a state of transition as I'm writing this. Hangouts On Air, which enabled live video broadcasts, has been shut down. That eliminates some great features that the remaining Hangouts do not offer. Google Hangouts still makes it possible to do a video chat with up to nine users, but the automatic recording and broadcast features died with Hangouts On Air. If you want to record your video calls, you're better off with Skype or similar products. Google is in the process of creating app-based products, so it will be interesting to see whether Hangouts gets a business makeover and eventually becomes a subscription app.

Google Drive is a winner. It's a cloud storage and sharing program that makes it very easy for you to store all kinds of digital materials on a virtual "drive." I would never recommend storing confidential or sensitive materials on Google Drive for security reasons, but for sharing documents, slide presentations, and files it works very well and being part of the Google product suite, it's ubiquitous. You control the sharing options and whether or not other people can edit or view. Google Drive is great for storing materials where they are easily accessible for work groups or teams.

Likewise, Google Docs works great for basic document sharing and limited content management, especially if your document is too large to e-mail as an attachment. It's a robust document creation program that is free and available to anyone with an Internet connection. Wisely, Google made Google Docs compatible with Microsoft Word. Google Docs have the advantage of being available in the cloud, so if you travel, you have access to your documents from wherever you are, even if you don't have your laptop with you. Templates and styling tools make it easy to put together nice-looking pages.

Although Google Docs is free, the more business-focused G Suite of products requires a monthly fee for an integrated set of useful applications. Google Sheets provides similar functionality for spreadsheets, whereas Google Forms takes care of surveys and Google Slides creates digital presentations. Google Sites makes it easy to create quick-and-easy intranet-style team sites to enable sharing and collaboration.

Google Translate is great for a casual translation of a phrase, but as many language students have discovered to their discomfort, it is no substitute for a good dictionary or a native speaker. Nuance, connotation, and idiom are often lost in translation, making for stories that are humorous unless they happen to you. You've been warned.

Gmail is here to stay. It's free and easy to set up, and ties into the Google suite of programs. Gmail is perfect for setting up alternative e-mail addresses to direct certain types of e-mails out of your main work or personal account or to set up a special-purpose e-mail address for a contest or landing page. You'll need at least one Gmail account to access the rest of the Google suite of products.

Google Calendar is a free calendar system that works well with Gmail and is accessible anywhere you can pull up Google. It integrates with Outlook and with scheduling systems like Calendly, and it's easy to set up and use. I wouldn't rely on anything provided by Google to be secure and private, but if you can live with that caveat, Google Calendar works well and provides a lot of features for a free program.

Google Maps are generally more accurate than your car's navigation system because they provide reliable, real-time updates on traffic conditions. You can get directions via a map, written instructions, or turn-by-turn vocal guidance. Because Google updates its maps more often than automakers refresh their navigation software, you're less likely to find your icon floating around in empty space when you travel on a relatively new stretch of road. Google Earth provides satellite views for almost everywhere on the planet. It's amazing in its ability to give you a bird's eye view of anywhere in the world and a little frightening with the ability to show your backyard to anyone who wants to look it up. Likewise, Google Street Views do a great job of taking you on a worldwide tour as if you're walking down a sidewalk anywhere the site's industrious photographers have canvassed (which is surprisingly far and wide).

Google Books scans public domain and publisher-permitted books for your specific search terms. That can come in handy for research. You can browse, borrow, and buy books as well.

Google provides well-integrated, reliable products that are either free or very reasonably priced. They're generally easy and intuitive to use, and provide functionality that used to only be available on enterprise-scale proprietary platforms for steep subscription fees. The cost of "free" software is privacy and the downside of easy sharing is security. Go into using Google's products as a wary consumer, and you'll find a lot to love.

THE LAST WORD

Check out what the Google suite of sites has to offer. Even if you don't choose to use any of the tools as your mainstay, it's helpful to have an account set up in case you find yourself on the road or away from the office and in need of services. Take advantage of the products, but protect yourself by keeping a backup elsewhere, just in case.

NEXT STEPS

1. Set up a Gmail account and start exploring the rest of the Google products.

2. Check out Google+ and see if enough of your tribe is on the site to make developing a presence worth your while.

3. Set up your Google Drive and practice moving a few files to get the hang of it.

4. Claim your YouTube channel name while you're logged into Google.

CHAPTER SIX

BLOGGING, PINTEREST, TUMBLR, AND INSTAGRAM

Blogging is a way to provide content on your topic of expertise in a way that is consistent and easy to find. That's very different from sites like Facebook and Twitter, where the primary goal is to be social. Although blogs do allow for comments and a degree of interaction, the conversation is not the main focus.

Text, videos, and photos are the main forms of blogging. Some bloggers do all three and upload the pieces separately to specialty sites or compile them together for more general platforms. So for example, you might have a WordPress blog where you can upload text-based posts, but you can easily embed a video or photos along with your text. Then, depending on the audience you want to reach, you could upload just the photos to a photo sharing site, and just the video to a video blogging platform.

How you blog depends on your audience's preferences, your type of content, and the time commitment you are able to make on a consistent basis. In this chapter, I'll share more about text and photo sites, and in the next chapter, we'll delve into Web video.

BLOGGING

Blogging is an essential part of being successful on social media. Your blog gives you a piece of Internet real estate that you "own" as much as that's possible online. Though all blogs rely on some kind of blogging software, you own the domain name (URL), and the major blogging platforms have been remarkably stable through time considering the general volatility of social media sites.

Many small businesses find that using a WordPress blog as the heart of their main Website provides a dependable solution that combines the best of both types of sites. A real benefit to this set-up is the ability for you to update your content at any time, and the fact that WordPress, one of the most popular blogging platforms, is well-maintained and frequently updated.

Another reason that WordPress tends to be the default platform for business is that its terms allow commercial use. Some other platforms, such as LiveJournal, are clear about wanting to remain noncommercial. Those sites are great if you're blogging about a hobby or passion, but don't try to use them for your business.

When most people talk about "blogging," they mean text-based posts. Your blog is a great way to share content, demonstrate your expertise, and gather your tribe. It's best to keep posts short—under 1,000 words and preferably around 500–750 words. Today's readers like information in easy, bite-sized formats. That doesn't mean you can't go more than the suggested word count (there's nothing to stop you), but recognize that readers who are confronted with pages of content may give up and move on without finishing. Generations raised on TV sound bites have carried a preference for "short and concise" into the blogging realm as well.

What should you blog about? Ask yourself what your target audience, your tribe, most wants to learn from you. Your blog is a way for people to get more information about you, your specialty, and your approach. It builds the like-know-trust factor. Don't be afraid to blog about your upcoming events and new products, but realize that your blog shouldn't be primarily an online sales platform. Talk about trending topics that relate to your specialty. Comment on books, news items, or events in a way that adds value for your readers. Tips, helpful information, insightful commentary, and even well-informed contrarian views can all serve to attract an audience.

Realize that your tribe has a large variety of options to learn about your subject matter. What will keep them coming back to your site are your voice and the unique personality and perspective you offer. If you have ever had a favorite news columnist or product reviewer, think about what it was that attracted you. Something about that person's approach to the topic clicked with you better than other sources. That "click" is what you're looking to create to keep your tribe coming back for more.

Ideally, you want to blog with relatively short posts on a consistent basis. Consistency builds your audience, because people look forward to hearing from you on a predictable schedule. For most people, it's harder to be consistent than it is to come up with things to write about. One way to get around that is by writing blog posts in advance and using scheduling software like Hoot Suite or Social Oomph to automatically update your site.

Where do you get your source material? Start with the articles you've written for other uses, cut them into parts or shorten them, and recycle them on your blog. You can also use points from speeches you've given, comment on something in the headlines that affects your industry or illustrates the value you provide, or react to an article or trending topic with your own perspective. Build your brand by making sure your content stays on topic for your area of expertise.

Invite other experts to be a guest on your blog from time to time. Pick people whose expertise complements yours without being competitive. Find people who can speak on related subjects to bring additional value. You gain credibility and influence by association when other notable experts share your platform (and the same is true when you are a guest on someone else's blog). Having interviews and guest bloggers also redirects some of the guest's audience and Web traffic to your site, and a percentage of them may decide to remain regular readers, helping you pick up followers.

Get the most value out of your blog posts by sharing them on your other social media sites. Share the links on Twitter and Facebook. Encourage your newsletter readers to follow your blog. If your blog and your Website are not one and the same, set up a feed so that your blog either automatically posts somewhere on your site or a link can take people from your site to your blog (there's usually a button to click for this). Consider getting even more traction out of your blog posts by making it easy to share your links via sites such as Social Buzz Club.

If you've created a body of original content for your blog, you may want to collect and organize related posts into a book. Or if you've already written a book, consider sharing excerpts and providing additional tangential material on your blog.

Break up your text with photos and video. Photos catch the eye and relieve the monotony of a gray block of words. Video adds movement and sound, creating a personal, welcoming touch and bringing a new immediacy to the written word. You can use bold type to highlight key points, drawing the reader's eye down through the text, making scanning more efficient. If you link to related content, blogs make it easy to embed the URL so it doesn't spoil the flow of the text.

Although blogs aren't primarily for conversation like Facebook, don't overlook the value of opening a dialogue with readers. Many bloggers like to end their post with a discussion question to draw out readers. Check back during the next 24–36 hours after your post goes live to respond to comments and engage readers. Reward readers by interacting with them and encourage additional comments by keeping the conversation going.

PHOTO SHARING AND BLOGGING

Photos get attention, and that's what you want online. Add a photo to your Facebook posts, blog posts, and Twitter tweets, and more people notice what you've said. When the photo is the most important thing you're sharing, consider sites like Pinterest, Tumblr, and Instagram.

Pinterest works like a giant bulletin board where you can sort photos by category and share them with friends. Its search capability allows you to look for more of the kinds of photo content you want to see, which you can then pin to your own boards and/or share to other social media channels.

Some of what you see on Pinterest are stand-alone photos, but many photos link to Websites to connect to articles, recipes, do-it-yourself instructions, and so on. Many people use Pinterest like a shopping wish-list or dream folder for everything from kitchen make-overs to wedding planning. If your photos are compelling, Pinterest users won't mind if the link takes them to a site where they can purchase what they see, but the photos need to be more interesting and have more personality than standard catalog fare.

Instagram is less about sorting the photos or arranging them into collections than it is taking and sharing pictures. Because the photos (as opposed to the grouping of photos) are the focus, Instagram offers more ability to add filters and other enhancements. It's less common for Instagram photos to link to other sites, so active selling doesn't work as well here. Consider building brand awareness with photos about your product's history, vintage/retro shots, behind-the-scenes photos, and even artistic portrayals. Make the photos striking, memorable, and unusual so people want to share.

Tumblr is a photo-blogging platform, meaning that it is set up to share photos and text, with the emphasis on the photos. That means you can share more of the story that goes with the photo on Tumblr than you can on Pinterest or Instagram, allowing you to create more context. Keep it short and sweet, and make the photo the star.

Regardless of where you share your photos, make sure to tag the images. Search engines can't "crawl" photos the same way they scan text, so they won't be able to read your logo in the photo. Tags and titles link descriptive words to your images to help search engines recognize the content. Titles are descriptive, as in "photo of a white wedding cake by Jane's Bridal," whereas tags are meant to grab the attention of search engines looking for specific queries. So the tag for the white wedding cake might be "weddings, wedding cakes, celebrations, Jane's Bridal, bride, reception, fondant, cake, #whitewedding." When in doubt, more tags are better than none.

What makes for good photo content? Eye candy. The more appealing and luscious the photo, the more attention you'll get. If you're sharing a recipe or a how-to, use step-by-step photos to illustrate your text. Before and after photos are especially compelling. If your business has visible results, use photos to convince viewers that the "after" you provide is a big, visible difference from the "before."

Consider showing your product in different seasonal, holiday, or situational settings. Or, theme the photos you post to the season or holiday to take advantage of people being "in the mood" for certain content. For example, if you sell housewares, show the same room or table setting decorated for different seasons, holidays, or types of gatherings. Give people ideas on how to use what they want or have in new ways and help them be more successful in using your product.

Pinterest photos tend to be pretty and straightforward. Instagram gets artsy. Tumblr gives you more room for explanation. Take those fundamental differences into account as you plan your strategy. It may not make sense for you to be on all three sites. Video is now supported on the sites as well as still photos, but make sure to take the audience into consideration as you plan your videos to be a good match for what they want from the site. Pinterest and Tumblr will be more receptive to how-to videos, whereas a video tour of a scenic setting might do better on Instagram.

Demographics also differ. Pinterest tends to skew a little older, whereas Tumblr skews more to those in their teens and 20s. Instagram gets more serious art and photography users. If you know the hobbies of your core audience and their interests beyond your product or service, you'll have insights that will serve you well in deciding which platforms to utilize and how to style your content.

All three sites are social media, so take advantage of the "social" aspect. Consider running photo-based contests where you encourage your customers to post and tag photos of your product in use. Reward them by acknowledging, sharing, and commenting on what they post. Retweet the best submissions to your Facebook business page and Twitter feed, acknowledging the contributors. Encourage conversation in the comments and get your customers talking about their experiences with your product, their new ways to use and maximize the items, or share tips and ideas. These are creative sites, so find ways for customers to have fun with your product and brand!

THE LAST WORD

Blogging is a great way to expand on your thoughts beyond a Facebook post. An active blog becomes an ongoing conversation that draws in readers and creates a dialogue to build relationships. Switch things up with photos and video. Take a break and put the spotlight on a guest now and then. Most importantly, make your blog fun and informative for both you and your readers.

NEXT STEPS

1. Check out the blogs for leaders in your field. Make note of how the sites are laid out, what topics they cover, and what kind of content they share.

2. Start thinking about the content you could use on a blog. Make a list of articles you've written that could be shortened and recycled, photos from events or your travels, and so on.

3. Sign up for a WordPress blog. The site has very good tutorials designed to make it user-friendly.

4. Check out Instagram, Pinterest, and Tumblr, even if you decide to wait before establishing a presence.

AN INTERVIEW WITH ELINOR STUTZ

In the following, LinkedIn and sales expert Elinor Stutz shares some insights on blogging:

Make the blog personal. I tell my story both on my blog and in my videos. Sales tips are included at the bottom of every blog. It is then distributed to major platforms where others share with their followings. Accordingly, thousands subscribe to the blog and this has led to collaborative projects. Strive to help your audience, as the reward is enormous.

My background is in corporate sales, which was highly competitive and the winning strategy secretive. However, upon becoming an entrepreneur, I realized the exponential power of collaboration.

I check in on social media three times a day and answer messages immediately. People ask to connect as they relate to what I have posted. Finding the common ground and interest leads to new opportunity.

My suggestion is to keep your profile up to date and easy to read, because most people are reading on their mobile phones.

I have many thousands of subscribers for my blog. The variety of platforms serves to attract entrepreneurs, corporate people, and media. It is posted on Facebook, LinkedIn, Twitter, and Google+. One big boost comes from a sales group where we reciprocate by posting each other's blogs. All combined, new subscribers join every day.

Chapter Seven

YouTube, Facebook Live, and Web Video

Welcome to the video generation. Video is rapidly becoming the preferred way to share information online, and it's never been easier. You've got a growing number of options for creating and sharing your video content, as well as ways to use Web video to grow your influence and extend your brand.

When the Internet started out, we felt very lucky just to share text-based messages, which seemed like a miracle in itself back in that long-ago time. Pictures and HTML changed everything, creating the highly visual Internet you know today. Streaming audio was next, quickly embraced by corporations, entrepreneurs, and speakers. Tools emerged to make it easy to record and share audio, leading to a booming growth in teleseminars.

Video initially posed a challenge due to bandwidth. But as technology changed, recording, uploading, and sharing video became easier. YouTube led the way, followed by other sites like Vimeo. For a while, the ability to easily produce Web videos outpaced the ease of sharing more than just the link to those clips.

Now that social media sites, blogging platforms, and e-mail newsletters have finally vastly improved the ability to embed video (to provide the now-common active video screen instead of just a link), the use of video is beginning to explode. It's a familiar, comfortable, and easily accessible format for viewers, who like being able to consume content while doing something else or perhaps just prefer to hear and watch rather than read. Major sites noticed the shift and are making it easier than ever to record and share your clips while increasing your reach.

Video dramatically increases the impressions and visibility of your social media posts. The combination of sight-sound-motion holds attention, and the combination of your face and voice creates a sense of intimacy and personal engagement that accelerates the like-know-trust cycle. The percentage of video content on the Internet increases every year, and experts say we're still at the early adoption point. Text-based posts aren't going to go away, but video is definitely a valuable weapon to have in your online arsenal.

Shorter is better. If possible, get your message across in 30 seconds, even if that includes a call to action to learn more from a Website. Viewership decreases as length increases unless the topic is of extremely high value and actively sought-out by the viewer. So someone might watch a five-minute video on how to change a flat tire or make a recipe because of the strong desire to learn the subject matter, but he or she is unlikely to watch a five-minute promotional video that randomly appears in the Facebook feed. Try to stay between 30 seconds and one minute unless you're sharing content that meets an urgent user need. Even with content that is part of a video course, realize that most people don't like to remain tied to their screen for more than five minutes, so break your content up into short, bite-sized pieces.

YouTube

YouTube is the granddaddy of video sites. It's where people turn first for entertainment and how-to videos, and given its enormous traffic, it's also the place to post your video in order to reach a huge, global audience.

Videos on YouTube can be available to the public, or restricted to a private audience. The site makes it simple to share with the major social media platforms, and serves up the code you need to embed a video on your blog or Website or share the video via e-mail. Many people aren't familiar with YouTube's easy video editing capabilities. Though not as robust as a full video editing suite like Microsoft Movie Maker or Apple iMovie, YouTube can still get the job done with the ability to make fundamental video and audio enhancements. You can add "cards" in the sidebar to take a viewer poll, or promote a Website or related video. Especially important is the ability to add subtitles and closed captioning.

Adding subtitles to your videos increases ease of use. Viewers can get the gist of the content even if they're in a location where they can't listen to audio. Hearing-impaired viewers aren't left out. Viewer engagement rises because they've got two elements to watch—the action on the video and the subtitle. Subtitles can also keep a Website or call to action in front of the viewer while you discuss related content.

YouTube is owned by Google, so it should be no surprise that it has its own powerful search engine running the site. That makes tagging your videos and writing keyword-specific video descriptions all the more important because you want your videos to be easily searchable and findable even by people who don't know exactly what they're looking for.

YouTube links share well on Twitter and embed easily on WordPress. But when it comes to Facebook, old rivalries die hard. Google and Facebook are long-time competitors, so although YouTube makes it easy to share videos on Facebook, Facebook's algorithms are rumored to be unfriendly to videos uploaded from YouTube.

YouTube has added a streaming capability with YouTube Live. Keep an eye on YouTube Live's developments.

FACEBOOK LIVE

Facebook Live is relatively new, but it's made a good debut. It's part of the Facebook phone app, and it makes it seamless to record video with your cell phone and upload direct to Facebook. One plus is simplicity, as Facebook Live removes the middleman of downloading a video to your computer in order to upload it to Facebook, or hoping that the camera's sharing capabilities load correctly.

The biggest win, however, is that Facebook appears to give preference in its algorithm to "native" video (video uploaded from Facebook Live or from your hard drive, that is, not from YouTube). Anecdotal evidence strongly suggests that Facebook exposes your native video posts to more people than the organic (unpaid) reach of your average post. The downside is that Facebook Live, at the time of this writing, doesn't make subtitles, cards, or other enhancements an option.

Here's how to get around Facebook's video bias. Use your cell phone to shoot a video and e-mail it to yourself (or use Dropbox or a similar file-sharing system). Download it onto your computer and add subtitles either in YouTube or in a program such as Windows Movie Maker. Save the subtitled file as an MP4 and upload it to your computer, then post the new "native" video to Facebook without the YouTube bias.

Facebook Live is valuable for making quick, slice-of-life videos on the go. If you know you won't get around to adding subtitles no matter their value, posting with Facebook Live and gaining the advantages of native video is much better than not doing video at all.

GOOGLE HANGOUTS

Google added Google Hangouts to its underperforming Google+, a live video feed that became immediately popular with entrepreneurs, coaches, and speakers. Google Hangouts makes it simple for up to 10 people to engage in a live, publicly visible video chat online. With a little effort, it's possible to screen-share, making it possible to present a slide show if you don't want to be on camera the entire time. For a while, Google Hangouts On Air made it easy to save your video to YouTube, but that capability was abruptly withdrawn. With Google+ languishing, speculation is rife about the future of Hangouts and whether it will remain a free public tool or be repurposed into a suite of business-oriented enterprise tools.

PERISCOPE, SNAPCHAT

Periscope is optimized for on-the-go as-you-are videos. The core idea was to make it easy to take and share live video of where you are in the moment and share it easily on Twitter.

Snapchat is very popular with the young adult crowd because it favors short video that is theoretically not saved or shared elsewhere, vanishing after a certain time interval. Savvy users realize that nothing online ever really goes away, but the ephemeral promise of Snapchat makes it a fun and trendy way to share in-the-moment observations and asides to build engagement with your audience.

Snapchat and Periscope have high intimacy because of the casual format. They're great for augmenting an established relationship with your most dedicated customers and followers, and lend themselves especially well to entertainment and lifestyle-oriented businesses.

GoToWebinar, WebinarJam, and Zoom

The programs I've talked about up to this point are great for casual chats, slice-of-life videos, testimonials, and product demos. But if you want to run true online events, you'll need something with more bells and whistles.

Skype can work for small meetings, but recording requires an add-on. The benefit from inclusive programs like GoToWebinar, Zoom, and WebinarJam comes in the all-in-one package. Features like a live chat capability for attendees during the Webinar, easy recording and download, the ability to screen share, switch who is controlling the screen, and have a host running the event behind the scenes all become increasingly important as your events scale in complexity and number of attendees.

Unfortunately, the Webinar platforms don't all offer exactly the same list of features, so you'll have to make trade-offs. You may be able to test-drive packages by being a guest on someone else's Webinar and seeing how easy (or difficult) the software is to use.

Factor in your own technological comfort level and level of frustration on event days to decide whether it's important for you to have a moderator. Think about how you want to store, share, and deliver your Webinar. Some programs can automatically share to YouTube, but make creating and saving an MP4 file difficult. Ideally, you want to be able to share and save the resulting video in a variety of ways.

Scalability matters. If you're just starting out, you want a program that can at least handle a couple of hundred attendees, and worry about trading up when you grow your following. If you've already got a substantial following, a large user base, or a big membership, look carefully at maximum capacity vs. price.

Some programs include the ability to create polls and handouts and to handle event registration. Although you can use multiple software packages to create those elements separately, it's nice not to have to keep switching among programs. Think about whether you want to use a separate platform to provide a dial-in phone number for the audio or whether you want phone/VoIP (Voice over Internet Protocol) to be inclusive with the Webinar package. The fewer separate pieces you or your moderator have to wrangle, the less stressed you'll be.

Another area where packages differ is in registration and promotion. Some packages focus only on the visual component, leaving you to handle registration through other programs. Others not only handle sign-ups but have built-in capability to create event landing pages, autoresponder e-mails to attendees, easy social media sharing, and sales tools like countdown timers and the ability to present a click-to-buy-now offer during the Webinar. Those capabilities might not mean as much if you are already using robust programs to do those things (and have staff to help you), but if you're a small organization or flying solo, it's nice to have all those elements integrated and easy to use.

Your choices on how to utilize Web video are wide and varied; there's something for every level of technology proficiency, audience taste, and personality. The popularity of video content and its success on social media means that video is here to stay, and utilizing it effectively is essential to growing your influence and brand. Lucky for you it's easier to do than ever before!

THE LAST WORD

Video is the future of social media. You don't have to be a rock star or a supermodel or a professional actor. Just get out there and do your thing, be yourself, and provide value. People with whom you might never cross paths will begin to feel like they know you and you will accelerate the like-know-trust progression. Once you get the hang of it, video is fun!

NEXT STEPS

1. Play around with video on your cell phone and laptop. (You can delete everything before it goes live, so no one will see you practice.) Get a feel for the features and controls.

2. If it makes you feel more confident, write down what you want to say and practice a few times before going on camera, but keep it natural and avoid sounding memorized.

3. Look for video opportunities in your everyday life. In your office, on the street, while traveling, making dinner, walking the dog, attending a conference—life is full of moments. Use video to share them.

4. Try subtitles. The first time or two might take a bit longer as you get used to the process, but once you figure it out, it goes quicker and gets easier!

5. Make video a part of your Facebook, tweets, LinkedIn, and blog. Keep it at 30 seconds to one minute, and have fun with it.

6. Make a promise to do video on your social media at least a couple of times a month. Or, jump in and go wild with it.

INTERVIEW WITH LOU BORTONE

Lou Bortone is an online video branding specialist and award-winning marketer. He is a former television executive who worked for E! Entertainment Television and later served as the senior vice president of marketing and advertising for Fox Family Worldwide, a division of Fox in Los Angeles. Lou is an author and ghostwriter of six business books, a Certified Guerrilla Marketing Coach, and a Book Yourself Solid Certified Coach.

Q: How has video led to a big shift on social media?

A: A lot more Internet traffic and content is video-driven than ever before. Video has become the preferred way we communicate, share entertainment, even the way we sell. Facebook prefers video. A lot of this is driven by the fact that people are on their phones. Fifty percent of YouTube videos are consumed on mobile devices. Younger viewers don't distinguish between consuming content on TV vs. phone.

We aren't abandoning the written word. It's just that our lives are so fast-paced that it's easier to watch instead of read. Bite-sized videos are easier than reading on a screen. People want to access what they want, when they want it, where they want, 24/7.

We are an always-on society with phones, tablets, constantly on and connected.

Q: How does the particular social media platform affect how someone might want to use video?

A: Social media platforms are constantly shifting. Facebook bought Instagram. LinkedIn bought Slideshare. Google Hangouts is changing. Facebook Live is becoming wildly popular. Connecting with your audience is key, but think about the message and the content, not just the platform. Think about the demographics of your audience and where they are using social media.

Who are you trying to reach and where are they using social media? Trying to chase people from one platform to another is a losing battle. Find your audience and reach them where they already are participating.

Q: How has social media changed the way business is done online?

A: Social media has connected us more and less. We do video e-mails instead of live sales calls. We have more opportunities to connect, but it doesn't mean we are connecting better. You can share the same content in a blog post or on Facebook Live, but the video gets much more engagement and greater reach.

Some people are more comfortable creating video than others. Facebook Live is less formal, good for shooting on the go. You can also do more formal videos. When you shoot on the go, it's more about getting the message out in the moment. Lighting and sound won't be as good. If there's a video that will have a long shelf life like on your Website, then take more time for quality on those branding videos. Take the time to do lighting and makeup and make it look good.

We may see some very pretty/charming people whose charisma is greater than their expertise. I'd like to think that content always wins over the pretty factor, but I'm not sure that's always the case. But we'll also see less polished people with real knowledge who can use slides and photo montages to get their point across. You have to think about your content and your delivery. We're all our own little TV stations now. Everyone with a cell phone is a broadcaster. This creates a responsibility to share good content. Information is easier to find than ever before.

We're seeing a gazillion little niches of people who want to explore their passions that may not be mainstream. We're living other peoples' lives vicariously.

Video accelerates the sales cycle because it builds the know-like-trust cycle faster. Video is more personal. People feel like they know you from your video, so it lets you connect in a more personal and engaging way.

Q: What should the average business person know about using video on social media?

A: Use video like you use e-mail. Grab your camera and record something short in the moment. It makes it really easy to communicate. Does that mean the message/content is as good because it's so easy? You still need to make sure your content is worthwhile.

Video is changing behavior. Everything is being seen now, which is making us more aware and cautious because it's harder for things to be hidden. We are thinking of our image and how we project ourselves. Video is great for exercising control over your brand. Every video you create is a building block for your brand. We are now more cognizant of our online image. We don't forget that cameras are everywhere. Cell phone videos record people behaving badly—it gets captured and shared.

How do you get normal people to get good at content and good at their message and up their game? Steve Martin said, "Be so good they can't ignore you." Play to your strengths. If the information you are sharing is valuable enough, what you look like doesn't matter.

Interview with Shawne Duperon, PhD

With her PhD in gossip, numerous Emmy awards, and social media reach topping 120 million per month, Dr. Shawne Duperon is considered by many to be one of the most innovative experts on communication today. Her case study, *Project Forgive,* was honored with a Nobel Peace Prize Nomination in 2016.

Q: How has social media changed video?

A: All the platforms like Facebook, YouTube, LinkedIn, they all reward video, especially video less than one minute long. It's a mental calculation we all make. If it's a long video, people don't want to take the time.

Video gets a large number of views. Make it worth people's time. Keep it at 59 seconds or less. We want to go where the party is, so the more views you have, the more views you'll get. Because the platforms reward video, we'll see more video. Use subtitles—they're eye candy.

We're really at the tipping point. It's been three years in the making. We're seeing Facebook Live, YouTube Live, Snapchat,

Instagram, Periscope, and the now-dead Blab. You don't have to be on all the platforms. Look at the demographics of your audience. Pick and choose the platform, and use video to help you capture e-mails.

Q: How is the video world reacting to the shift from broadcast to cable to Netflix to streaming video?

A: It's really adapt or die. Broadcast stations are now dabbling in streaming video. We used to listen to someone in a position of authority—the old broadcast stations. Now, they're on equal ground on social media. This generation doesn't react well to people on a pedestal. Reporters in their online persona don't work well on social media. Entertainers and celebrities work very well.

A "regular person" can get plenty of traction. You don't have to be a celebrity or an actor. Live video doesn't have to be good (from a production standpoint), just authentic and good content.

When we were shooting the *Project Forgive* documentary, we put up clips and teaser videos with subtitles. The key is keeping it short. Once you build a following, you can go longer.

Facebook Live is like a radio show. You can go 20–30 minutes and interview guests. Keep acknowledging and showing appreciation for your guests. Constantly reiterate the topic for people who just joined in. Sharing causes video to go viral, where you'll reach a larger audience than what you'll reach live. You can also use Facebook Live during a real-time speech, so you're reaching two audiences at once.

The key is to post your video on your business page and not your personal page. Gossip theory holds that you will only get a limited number of views, so post it on your business page to cause engagement, and then share it to your personal and other pages. Other people will share it also, and that creates momentum through your tribe. You know you're doing well by the quality of your comments. On a business feed, people will start sharing personal experiences and stories.

Have the camera at eye level so you don't make people feel inferior or talked down to. Be close to the camera. Social media is about intimacy. Use the word "you." Act like you're talking to one person. Video quality doesn't have to be stellar, but audio must be great. Most people aren't even going to notice if you screw up. Don't take long to get into the meat of what you're saying. If you take more than five or six seconds, people leave.

Close with some kind of action—ask them to like, share, comment, thumbs up on YouTube (which is really important for SEO [search engine optimization]).

Your best reach is organic reach. People spend time on Facebook selling and they should be using quotes, pretty pictures, and video.

Create a level of trust before sharing articles. Don't just share your quotes, but share ones by major people like Nelson Mandela, etc. You'll grow into being "famous" over time.

Respect copyright. Don't just grab pictures from Google to use. That violates copyright. Make your own posters. Or share from the original site, which keeps the attribution. Create energy by sharing from other pages that have the same energy you want to create. Tap into their reach and algorithm when you share their content. Comment on the original post that you are "sharing at site name," which creates a cycle of reciprocity for them to re-share.

The larger the following of the page from which you're sharing content, the more impact you get from sharing.

Post as often as you want on your business page (not profile). No one will complain unless the posts don't resonate or they're poor quality.

Take risks. Share from the heart. Be uncomfortable. You can always dial it back. Talk about overcoming failure. Realize that if you're always sharing your wins, it can make other people feel bad. Don't brag. It's okay to share a mix of good and regular news.

— SECTION THREE —

LEVEL UP YOUR GAME

CHAPTER EIGHT

MAXIMIZING INTEREST SITES, MEETUP, REDDIT, AND FORUMS

When most people talk about social media, they mean Facebook, Twitter, LinkedIn, and sites like Tumblr and Instagram. Even blogs often get left off the mental checklist. Yet there's a much larger world of social media sites waiting for you, and all of them focus on the "social" part—facilitating conversations. They all have their special focus, audience, and capabilities, but some are likely to be perfect for helping you extend your influence and build your brand.

INTEREST AND INDUSTRY SITES

If you belong to a trade or professional association or a special-interest club, odds are high there's a Website. Especially for larger groups, it's also very likely that the site includes some level of forum, bulletin board, or discussion group capability. These are all places to meet new people, open conversations, demonstrate your credibility, and gather your tribe.

Many forums within membership sites work a lot like Facebook posts. Someone begins a thread with a question, and related answers nest beneath that opening post. If it's a professional membership site, you're assured to find either colleagues or potential clients. Make yourself accessible and useful. Answer other people's questions, and take the initiative to open the conversation by posting starter comments of interest to much of the audience. Some sites have a culture of active online discussion, whereas others may need you to get things going. Hang in there. Even if you only attract a small audience at first, you are sharing useful information and demonstrating expertise, as well as gathering a tribe.

Use the site's member directory to seek out people who might be good contacts and invite them to join the conversation. Ask their opinions and solicit their input. Interview them. If you can invigorate on-topic discussion, you'll become a hero to the site organizers, and you're likely to find that you've become a minor celebrity at the next in-person meeting from the number of people who recognize your name from online.

Observe etiquette when you're interacting in an online forum. Keep the discussion focused on topics appropriate to the setting, and gently but firmly manage your threads to keep out blatant self-promotion, spamming, bad behavior, and tangents. Be as professional online as you would be in person, treating everyone with respect, keeping a civil attitude, and not allowing louder voices to drown out other perspectives.

Don't go onto the forums to get a quick sale. That will backfire. Go to be a good member and to get to know your colleagues. Mention your experience or credentials when it's relevant, but don't come on too strong. Make sure your member profile represents you well and includes how to contact you outside of the site. It's amazing how many people never fill out their profiles, making it impossible for others to get in touch or validate their expertise.

Networking in membership and special-interest sites is a long-term strategy. In the offline world, it can take months or years to begin to get sales from attending meetings and mixers for an organization. People need time to like, know, and trust you. Savvy business people don't expect to get referrals the first time they show up, although it can happen. Instead, pick your sites wisely and make a commitment to be a regular participant, just like in the "real" world.

Some organizations create private LinkedIn or Facebook groups instead of hosting their own password-protected forum on their Website.

If that's the case, all the same rules just discussed apply. Stay out of arguments, always be polite, and stick to the topic at hand. You will be welcome and remembered positively if you are always helpful.

REDDIT

Reddit is a massive site with forums dedicated to almost any topic possible. It's got a huge user base, and can be a great way to connect with people who share common interests. You can start your own dedicated topic page (called a subReddit) or participate in an existing page. It's always easier to get to know how a site works by beginning as an observer on someone else's page, so I'd recommend spending time to get to know the "neighborhood" before trying to start your own subReddit.

Like all online communities, Reddit has its own personality, rules, and culture. In particular, Reddit users don't like to be sold-to unless it is on a subReddit specifically for self-promotion. (Realize that the chance anyone is going to those pages to buy is exceedingly slim. They're really a holding area to segregate promotional posts so they don't disrupt the real conversation. Don't waste your time.)

Reddit is a combination forum and bulletin board. You can post links to interesting on-topic information you've found elsewhere and invite discussion (just don't pin your own posts unless they're about a topic instead of about you). You're safest sharing links to other people's excellent articles and blog posts and then steering the conversation that ensues. There's also nothing to stop you from having someone else (an assistant or colleague) post links to your content (so it isn't being posted by you), but don't overwhelm the thread. You want to be present consistently enough to be noticed, but not so much that you dominate.

Be on your very best behavior. The personality of Reddit users varies by subReddit, but in general it is a bit rough and tumble, and when community norms are violated it's downright hostile. If LinkedIn is the white-table restaurant of the Internet and Facebook is the local diner, Reddit is more like the corner bar. Don't go looking for a fight, don't give anyone reason to bring the fight to you, and you'll probably have a great time and meet cool people.

MEETUP

Meetup makes it easy to gather people with similar interests for live, local events. The site is inexpensive and easy to use, and once you post your event (unless you change default settings) it is visible to all Meetup members, who can then RSVP online. Once users "join" your page, you can e-mail them individually or as a group.

Recurring events are Meetup's strong suit. It's perfect for starting a discussion group, promoting club meetings, or raising the visibility of in-store or live events. As the group organizer, you can approve or disapprove membership requests, charge a fee to belong to the group, and even manage sponsors.

Meetup lets a group organizer upload files or photos to share with members and create polls. The membership list can be downloaded, so you can capture e-mail addresses to use with your newsletter. Meetup also shows you what other groups are most popular with your members, which is a great way to identify places where you might find future members. If your topics are compatible, you might even approach organizers of other local Meetups to do occasional joint events. At the least, you may want to attend some of the "also popular with" groups to meet new prospects.

It's easy to invite Facebook friends to your Meetup thanks to a helpful internal app, as well as to link your Outlook address book. The most powerful benefit lies in how easy it is for new people to find your Meetup if you've placed it in the appropriate category and described it compellingly. Focus on the benefit to members in your description to encourage new sign-ups. Utilize the ability to discuss the topic in the body of the event post, and encourage your members to rate the events afterward and post evaluations, which provides even more incentive for new people to try out the group.

Whichever sites you choose to frequent, consistency and helpfulness are key. Be a good neighbor; give people reason to like, know, and trust you; and build relationships before you try to land business. In other words, do all the same things online that you've been doing in the offline world to maximize your brand and grow your influence!

THE LAST WORD

In a way, social media actually requires better conversational skills than real life, because you don't have nonverbal cues or facial expressions to ease the way. When you connect with people on an online forum, remember your best manners, aim for clarity to avoid misunderstandings, and do your best to be helpful. Once you get into the swing of things, you might discover that interacting in forums is not only useful, but actually enjoyable.

NEXT STEPS

1. Explore the Websites for your professional and interest associations. Look for forums and conversation threads. Spend time lurking before you dive in so you understand the site etiquette.

2. Think about what value you can bring to discussions on the various forums in which you're interested. How can you answer questions, add knowledge, or provide perspective?

3. Go slow. Test the waters by answering a few questions or commenting on someone else's thread and gradually work up to more. Don't burst on the scene by showing up in every conversation.

4. Be alert for good content by other people that you can share links to on sites like Reddit and elsewhere which will provide value to readers (and build goodwill with content creators).

Chapter Nine

Internet Radio and Podcasting

Back in the old days, radio signals broadcast through the air, and you listened on an honest-to-goodness radio. Internet radio—and its cousin, podcasting—fulfill the same function, but use different technology. They use computers and the Internet, and because there's no real "broadcast" involved and thus no FCC, it's opened up radio to a whole new generation of hosts and audiences, expanding far beyond what AM/FM and satellite radio ever imagined. Sometimes referred to as "Webcasting" and sometimes as "Internet streaming radio," we're talking about the same thing, radio you can listen to through the Internet on your phone, tablet, or computer.

It's easier than ever for someone with a good message and the gift of gab to reach a worldwide audience, without the need for a broadcast license, frequency assignment, expensive equipment, transmitter, or any of the old barriers to entry that used to keep radio locked up in the hands of a few.

By way of definition: when I talk about "streaming Internet radio," I'm referring to a live broadcast. "Podcasting" can refer to either archived (recorded) episodes of a show that was originally broadcast live, or pre-recorded shows that are released on a schedule. There are pluses and minuses for both, which we'll explore. Both Internet radio and podcasting can be a fantastic way to grow your audience and influence while creating and extending an indelible brand.

Blog Talk Radio

Out of all the Internet radio sites that come and go, Blog Talk Radio (BTR) is the granddaddy. It's the place to find hundreds of shows on all kinds of topics, from business to lifestyle, and through the years, the site has refined its technology to make live streaming radio easy and inexpensive.

When Internet radio and podcasting began, producing a good show required a set-up worthy of a small radio station, including microphones and soundboards. In the decades since then, not only have computers and software gotten much more sophisticated when it comes to recording capabilities, but so have sites like Blog Talk Radio. If you decide to get into Internet radio in a big way and make your living from sponsored shows, you might want to eventually consider upgrading your equipment. But the beauty of Internet radio is that you can get your feet wet and start building an audience without investing in special equipment.

An all-in-one site like BlogTalkRadio.com has got you covered. BTR has an online "studio" that makes it easy for you to host your shows. When you produce your show through BTR, they take care of the technical stuff such as hosting and servers. All you need to get started is a laptop with a good microphone and a high speed, reliable Internet connection. BTR makes it easy to live stream and to record your shows and archive them, then promote them via social media and upload them to sites like iTunes. When you're getting started, having a one-stop site that integrates seamlessly with all of those functions means you can focus on creating great content, gaining finesse as a host, and growing your audience.

Because BTR is an established hub, your show becomes immediately easier to find. They've got measurement capabilities built in, as well as the ability to integrate paid advertising into shows and to create monetization streams for podcasts. Many listeners looking for new shows go to BTR first. It's a great way to get up and running and get noticed without having to become a tech geek.

One of the most exciting things about Internet radio is that without the high costs of entry for traditional radio, anyone with a passion for a topic, a computer, and a good Internet connection can have a show, no matter how niche the audience. Because the production costs are so low, it's up to you whether you plan to eventually make money off your show through advertising and sponsorships, or do it as a labor of love (and promotion).

Self-help is a big topic for Internet radio, but business shows are also very popular, along with financial issues, empowerment, current events, religion, and lifestyle issues. Think about your area of expertise, the brand you want to build, and the audience you want to attract, and then consider the types of topics and guests you would be most comfortable hosting. Decide whether your commitments and preferences lend themselves to being in front of a microphone and a live audience at the same time on the same day each week, or whether you'd be better off pre-recording shows when time permits for scheduled distribution (podcasting).

If you discover that being a radio host is what you were born to do (or just that you're good at it and enjoy it), you can trade up to sites like BBSradio.com that offer live engineered remote Internet broadcasting and hosting. BBS takes the do-it-yourself out of Internet radio, giving you the virtual studio crew to produce an even more professional product. As with BTR, BBS does both live streaming radio and pre-recorded podcasts, and also enables recording the live shows as podcasts and syndicating them to increase exposure. Unlike BTR, BBS will also handle sound levels, call-ins, and running preproduced commercials, as well as post-broadcast editing.

Both BTR and BBS have social media capabilities built in. They make it easy to upload links to new shows on Facebook, Twitter, LinkedIn, and other sites and offer the capability for live interactive chat boards. BTR also has a Facebook-like comment capability on shows in their archive. These capabilities open up opportunities for hosts to really interact with their audiences on the main site where those conversations become part of the show's advertising and build the like-know-trust factor.

Many if not most hosts will also create a Facebook page for the show, and integrate it into their Website. If you make the commitment of becoming a radio show host, you want maximum visibility for your show. That means advertising your show through social media to gather listeners and attract potential sponsors who can underwrite your show and provide a stream of in-bound advertising income. Highly successful shows with large audiences and strong sponsorship can become a full-time paying job for the host.

PODCASTING

The name "podcasting" dates back to the time when indie recorded shows would be listened to on an iPod. Times and technology have changed, but the name stuck.

As mentioned earlier, "podcasting" can either refer to episodes of a previously live-streamed show that have been recorded and archived for download, or shows that are intentionally pre-recorded for later distribution.

Podcasting has enjoyed a recent surge in listenership because the episodic on-demand nature of the media suits today's lifestyles. Listeners can catch an episode during their daily commute, or listen all day at work depending on the job. Unlike live radio, podcast episodes are always available, so there's no need to work around a broadcast schedule.

Shows can range from five minutes long to an hour or more, depending on the type of content and listener interests. Some podcasts feature a single host discussing themed topics, but many shows feature one or more guests, as well as listener call-ins.

In addition to BTR and BBS, Libsyn is one of the long-time best sites for podcasters. Libsyn (originally short for "liberated syndication") is a podcasting hosting and distribution site. It has excellent integration with social media and syndication platforms, as well as a podcast app for mobile users, making it easy to store and distribute your podcast, and it offers hosting packages in a variety of price points. You don't get the bells and whistles that come with BTR and BBS, but if you're already experienced with the production aspects and just need a good hosting or distribution site, Libsyn is worth a look.

Not only do podcasts cater to the same range of interests as streaming Internet radio, but there are other niches that have found a welcoming home in podcasting. Many fiction authors have embraced podcasting to produce serialized audio dramas, either with a single narrator or with a full cast of characters like the old-time audio dramas. Fans of TV shows and sports can live their dreams of creating a never-ending discussion and analysis of their favorite topics with a dedicated listener base. Whether it's cooking, crafts, do-it-yourself projects, or something else, if you're passionate about a topic, podcasting might be a perfect way to connect with others who love what you do. That following might be the launch of a brand new career. Your show's structure is limited only by your imagination.

THE LAST WORD

Think about your content and your time commitments, as well as your comfort level in front of a microphone. If you haven't already been a guest on someone else's Internet radio show or podcast, pitch to some that dovetail with your topic and see what it's like. The podcasting community in particular is a welcoming place, so get to know some experienced hosts and ask questions. Look for a niche, check out the competition, and give it a shot!

NEXT STEPS

1. Explore BTR, BBS, and similar sites. Compare pricing and services to get a feel for what might be right for you.

2. Listen to some of the shows, look at what's being offered in your niche, and think about what you could do to bring a fresh perspective.

3. Make a list of possible topics and guests. Think about what kind of format you would want for your show—single-host, multi-host, call-in, etc.

4. Be realistic about how much time you can allot on an ongoing basis. If your schedule varies, consider prerecording podcasts rather than live weekly broadcasts.

5. Reach out to shows as a potential guest, and get to know hosts to explore your questions.

INTERVIEW WITH DEBBI DACHINGER

Debbi Dachinger is a media personality who has been interviewed on more than 700 media outlets. She is a syndicated, award-winning radio host and producer, interviews celebrities on the red carpet, is an on-camera event host, keynote speaker, a certified coach, and author of internationally best-selling books.

Q: How has social media impacted Internet radio?

A: I think we've proven that Internet radio is here to stay. There's an amazing force of listeners, and the listening audience has doubled every year. Listeners tuning in have engaged en masse.

Social media has allowed audiences to tap into the online radio and podcast resources available. It made a new way of giving Internet radio viable breadth and life.

People are less interested in receiving e-mail newsletters. The way people tune in is social media: Twitter, LinkedIn, Facebook, Twitter ads, personal RSS feed. We have an indigenous RSS feed for the show that auto-populates into the biggest podcast sites. Google Alerts let me see when it goes viral. It also goes out through all my social media, different headlines, different visuals, rolling out over and over.

Hashtags let people know what's trending and tap into the news. When you align with what's going on in the world, you draw massive attraction and attention.

Q: How has social media changed how people listen to radio?

A: The show has to be good. You have to pay attention to your audience numbers. There is a lot of competition and that forces you to up your game. You need to know, what is your niche? Be specific, brand yourself. Bring your unique point of view and unique personality. It's okay to be funny as well as to have a strong point of view. Through social media, you can reach out to local groups, and you shine your light on listeners, drawing them in.

Q: Radio stations use live events to promote shows. How does social media get involved?

A: Our Internet radio station is a hub. It creates activity all over social media; content leads back to the site and the on-air shows. It's a spider web of activity on social media that goes back to the station, our sponsors, the personality of the station, and its programs.

Being interactive on social media is huge. People love it when you ask for their opinions. Surveys are great. Get opinions on topics and use it to build the show. Give listeners a way to comment. Get them to share their thoughts on the topic and their interests; give them a way to offer feedback.

Social media creates an unprecedented degree of interaction and listener control. They have ultimate control, because without listeners, you have no show. I'm always looking for ways for them to direct our content, bring them in, keep people engaged and interested.

Facebook is huge. I've booked clients for my outside business through people who have requested coaching and help on LinkedIn, Twitter, or Facebook, and I've filled workshops, created brand preference. It doesn't matter what works for others; cater to what works for your audience. Knowing this is a leg up and enormous.

When you put something out there to the public, write a headline that's creative and exciting, full of action, something that makes people care. Make the content mysterious and intriguing. Use photos.

Create a stream that tells more about the story you're telling. Connect with your station beyond podcasting. Most stations will retweet your tweets, and has everything built into a station's platform, such as keeping your program's archive.

Social media is an invaluable tool for radio and podcast promotion; free and easy to use, it's an unbeatable way to connect with your listeners and gain publicity for your program. However, to ensure that your social media efforts make an impact, it's a good idea to create a strategy.

It is good to announce what's playing on your social media platforms. The occasional "now playing" tweet will give potential listeners a flavor of your program, and encourage them to tune in. If you want detailed feedback on specific elements of your show or station, create a poll on Twitter or Facebook where listeners can vote on subjects.

If you want to get your audience involved, give listeners a chance to shape the show by encouraging them to request their favorite guests, songs, or conversation via Facebook or Twitter. You could do this on an ongoing basis, or allocate times of the day when listeners can take over the show.

Giveaways are a fantastic way to generate exposure. Encourage brands to donate prizes for your competitions, or get creative with fun or unusual prizes that won't break the bank. Why not pass on those guest passes you were sent by the press company, instead of keeping them for yourself? By enabling listeners to enter by sharing or retweeting your post, you can grow your reach and attract new listeners.

If you have big ambitions for your Internet radio show, it's crucial to find a viable way to generate a regular income. Social media is a fantastic tool for seeking sponsorship, making it relatively simple to add value to your sponsors if you have a good following. By creating a sponsorship package that includes a detailed social media plan, you're far more likely to seal a deal.

Social media is a quick and easy way to gain feedback from your listeners, to help you refine and improve your program.

Q: **If you're taking cues from the listeners, how do you keep your show's purpose and content from getting onto tangents from your original purpose?**

A: To be a successful radio personality or podcast host, you've got to retain an authentic voice and message, regardless of what you hear from listeners. But it's also important to validate listeners via social media and on air by mentioning them on air, mentioning what they've told you. I'm always following up on comments and tweets, posting videos. It's fun, frivolous. I love Facebook Live. It's a great way to target key listeners that you most want to attract.

You've got to know who your people are, support the causes they're passionate about, connect with listeners and their friends.

I talk about people on air who write to me, talk about what's trending, mention listeners by name. Listeners who interact can voice what others don't have the courage to ask. Opinions go viral.

Through social media, a radio or podcast host can create prizes for loyal listeners with acknowledgment by you and the station. It's important to create opportunities to get listeners engaged and keep people involved in what we do.

We keep bits of fun and crazy in the show. People will follow you if you're fun. We make our listeners feel loved, smarter, appreciated, like there's a feeling of being connected, being home.

Q: **How can new hosts figure out what's right for them, radio or podcast?**

A: Podcasting and radio are two different mediums for conveying the same type of content. First, podcasts are free from clock constraints. Unlike a radio show, a podcast doesn't have to time out to a specific length, it doesn't have to meet breaks at specified times, and hosts don't have to reset the conversation every five minutes to let people who are just tuning in know what they're listening to. Nobody tunes in to the middle of a podcast.

Next, most radio shows need to try to please a lot of people at once. Podcasts, in contrast, can serve people with the same peculiar interest or taste who are united by the magic powers of the Internet and form the core of 20,000-plus people who collectively make a podcast commercially viable.

Last, podcasts, as accessed by most consumers, are things that listeners "opt in" to. Instead of just flipping on the radio and either loving or hating what they hear, podcast listeners usually find things they like and commit to them by subscribing. This results in a different relationship between the content creator and the audience.

Digital content is radio's present and future. Much like television, where more and more people are consuming video via YouTube, Amazon, Netflix, and DVRs, many are listening to audio at a time of their choosing.

TV has seen a decline in viewing as people self-curate, using their smartphones and other digital devices. Radio is experiencing a similar arc of change. This is largely driven by Millennials.

Podcasts, while a natural extension for radio broadcasters, are intrinsically different than radio in some important ways.

Radio is great at putting together a sportscast, sequencing music, generating newscasts with correspondents from all over the world. Push the button and radio does it all. Podcasts, on the other hand, are "opt-in." Consumers must find and then choose to download a podcast. The intent is very different.

On radio, the show is always "on." People tune in and tune out all the time. They either like what they are hearing or move on. In podcasting, everyone has the common experience of starting at the beginning. Which, of course, is no guarantee that the content will keep them engaged.

Radio is a button push away. Podcasting requires opt-in. In podcasting, listeners must find, select, and in most cases, download a program. The hurdle is higher. But so is the listener engagement.

Audio content creators need to be aware that traditional radio and podcasting are more than just different distribution technologies. While they share much in common, they are in most ways two different media—each with their own unique quirks.

Podcasts are very popular, and like being on radio, you must be good at it to gain a loyal audience. It's a smart move to find a mentor and get coached up front so you are spectacular from the start and have a short learning curve. You want to build a following right away. You've got to know your brand, audience, and niche. Do something you love.

CHAPTER TEN

KICKSTARTER, PATREON, AND GOFUNDME

The Internet is not a bank or an ATM. Just posting something—even something really cool—online will not automatically make strangers throw money at you. Yet the Internet has managed to turn the way we handle money inside out and upside down in a variety of ways.

Most of us at least access our bank and financial accounts online even if we cling to getting a paper statement in the mail. Likewise, paying bills online is the norm more than the exception. We send and receive money via PayPal without batting an eye. So it might not really be so strange that the Internet has also democratized angel investing and the centuries-old model of being a true patron of the arts.

Kickstarter, Patreon, and GoFundMe are three of the best-known funding platforms, but they are vastly different in their structure and purpose. Other sites like these exist, but these three are the best known and most successful, at least at the time I'm writing this book. Whether or not they will work for you depends on what you're trying to accomplish and how hard you're willing to work for it.

Whole books have been written about how to run a crowdfunding campaign. I'm only going to touch on a few essentials. First, have a good product. Enthusiasm won't make up for shoddy goods. Second, do your homework and due diligence about your development and manufacturing costs, production essentials, packaging, shipping, handling, and fulfillment plans. Many a successfully funded project has come to grief because the campaign manager did not accurately figure out what it would take to actually produce the product (or forgot to charge for shipping and handling). The horror stories are legendary, and you don't want to be a new one, so make a business plan, just like you would in the offline world, and consult people who have successfully crowdfunded similar products. The creator community is remarkably open, friendly, and helpful when approached seriously and with respect. Ask for and take advice from people who have done this before. And third, plan for heavy, ongoing promotion.

Just putting up a campaign page will not send money flowing to your door, regardless of which platform you choose. It takes work to design a good campaign, and it requires time and commitment to gain the trust of the platform's community in advance of a campaign. Promoting the project requires constant, consistent effort utilizing as many social media sites as you can manage. It is not a one-person job. In fact, one hallmark of successful campaigns is that they have a dedicated (nearly obsessive) team behind them to share the work and leverage the online following of multiple creators.

Having been part of quite a few successful Kickstarters, I can attest that the promotional volume and frequency borders on overkill, but it's essential, especially in the crucial first few and last few days. It can also be fun. Being online with friends and interacting about every new pledge in real-time has the feel of one of those PBS phone-a-thons. It became addictive watching the funding level inch upward, exhorting our followers on social media to get in on the deal before it ended.

The beginning and ending of a campaign are when most of the money comes in. Good campaigns don't appear out of nowhere and expect an immediate influx of backers. Smart project managers let their core audience know a campaign is coming well in advance, stoking interest and desire, dangling tidbits about the rewards and stretch goals, and revealing glimpses before the campaign goes live. The goal is to have a large group of enthusiastic backers ready to jump in as soon as the project is open to create a surge of interest.

Projects that fund rapidly in the first crucial days attract attention. They're more likely to become a Kickstarter "staff pick" or be featured as a hot project where they'll catch the eye of backers looking for a good deal. That's why getting that momentum early is so essential, and why good prepromotion and heavy initial communication about the campaign is nonnegotiable.

Most campaigns sag a bit in the middle, a reason to structure the length to be about a month, give or take a bit, so that the project doesn't become old news. Backers will straggle in, and now it becomes important to have good pre- and post-funding milestone goals so that there is always something new and exciting to tell your audience and backers. Ideally, you always want to be just closing in on a new milestone with extra rewards or just celebrating passing a goal to keep the campaign exciting.

Make sure your partners in the campaign understand the relentless nature of the promotion necessary to succeed. Not everyone will see every post or tweet (remember what I said about the organic views on Facebook being in the low single digits), so you've got to talk about it a lot, and visibility rises in the algorithm the more people you tag and who like, comment, and share your posts. Get your echo chamber on board in advance.

The last few days of a campaign are the final surge. It's possible in Kickstarter to tag a live project to remind you when it's near the end of its run, so backers can decide at that point whether or not to jump in. Some people love swooping in with the final dollars that push a project over its threshold. Others will make a minimum pledge early on, and come back later to see if they can nudge the needle to achieve an attractive stretch goal, or put in more money for a reward level once they're reasonably sure the campaign will fund.

If you eased up at all on your promotion in the middle, it's time to kick it up a notch to cross the finish line. Remember to communicate with your backers too, encouraging them to bring their friends into the deal. The last few hours can feel like a party on social media, or a bender in Vegas, pulling the lever on the slot machine and hoping to ring up a win. Plan to be online the whole time on all your social media sites during the last few hours and make it as interactive, engaging, and fun as possible to woo the last few backers. Nothing succeeds like success, so brag a little about what you've achieved if you're past the base amount and super-funding. Or, beg shamelessly (and endearingly) if you're in the last stretch and not quite there, reminding potential backers of all the project benefits plus any incentives that have been unlocked.

Remember that no matter what tangible product your campaign delivers, your backers have plenty of other ways they could get a similar item elsewhere. The thrill of crowdfunding for the backer is bringing something to life, being part of a group with a purpose, and getting a good deal with extra rewards and freebies. In other words, the social aspect of crowdfunding is addictive and is part of what is being purchased. Make it an event and consciously build up anticipation, excitement, anxiety, and celebration.

KICKSTARTER

Kickstarter is the gold standard for crowdfunding sites. It's a site for makers and creators to post a campaign in order to raise money to bring a project to life. The types of projects vary widely. Exploding Kittens, a memorably named tabletop card game, raised more than $8.7 million from more than 200,000 backers, setting a record. *Athena's Daughters*, an anthology about heroic female characters written by female authors, raised more than $44,000 from almost 2,000 backers and became the most successful anthology on the site at that time.

I backed Exploding Kittens, and I was one of the anchor authors in *Athena's Daughters*, as well as being an author-participant in a number of other successful Kickstarters. No matter how it might appear to outsiders, crowdfunding is not "free money." Good campaigns don't happen by accident, and campaign managers work hard for months before, during, and after a campaign to make a project successful.

Kickstarter's premise is simple. The person in charge of the campaign posts a description of the product to be funded and how the money will be used. Usually, this includes incentives and rewards for backers to exceed the minimum level of funding. Projects that overfund deliver extras to their backers, all spelled out in the project description.

The video at the top of a project page is essential. Skimp on quality or create a video that doesn't accurately capture your campaign's purpose, and most potential backers won't read further. It doesn't have to be Hollywood-level slick, but it does need to convey competence, professionalism, and heart. Here's a place where branding and credibility really matter, and come into play in a big way.

Don't rush into creating a Kickstarter campaign. Spend time on the site looking at similar projects to the one you want to run. See what works and what doesn't. Study the failures as well as the successes. Back campaigns. Kickstarter is a community as much as it is a crowdfunding platform, and backers want to know that you support other creators. Most campaigns offer backer levels for as low as $1 or $5, so you can afford to participate in several campaigns to get the feel for how things really work.

Your campaign page should be easy to understand. Backers should be able to tell by skimming the page what your base funding level is, what the product being funded is, and what backers at various levels of funding will receive. Building backer trust is essential. You're asking strangers to give you money to underwrite creating a product, so you need to make sure that every aspect of your page gives them a reason to trust you. Showing that you've been active backing other projects is a step in the right direction. A good video that features you, the creator, is another step, as is a well-written and easy-to-follow campaign page.

Communication is key. Kickstarter has a built-in mechanism for the project owner to communicate with backers. Use it. One of the biggest complaints backers voice is receiving too little communication from the creator of the project, especially if delivering the product hits delays. They will forgive a well-explained delay, but leaving them hanging in silence is likely to kill your prospects of doing another successful campaign. Increase your influence by nurturing your relationship with backers.

Kickstarter is social. Backers can comment on the campaign and want to hear from you, the creator. Gaining the coveted status of having your project become a "staff pick" gives your campaign visibility, likely to attract backers who consider window shopping on Kickstarter and making impulse purchases to be a fun way to spend an evening. Much of your project's funding may come from people who don't know you or your company outside of the campaign. But once they back your project, you begin to build an audience that can follow you from one project to another, because you have a backer list and permission to contact them about other projects of interest. As with your e-mail list, treat your backer list with care. Don't be afraid to contact them about new projects, but never spam them. "List fatigue" is a real hazard, so make your communications count.

Indiegogo is the other big crowdfunding site. It works much like Kickstarter with some important exceptions. One is that Indiegogo permits fundraising for charitable causes, which Kickstarter no longer allows. Indiegogo is also getting into the business start-up funding market, bringing the crowdfunding model to equity investment, a brand new feature. There's a lot to like about Indiegogo, but one downside is important. Historically, Indiegogo's user base has not been as large as Kickstarter's. Because a lot of the support for projects on Kickstarter come from strangers, people who were out browsing on the site and happened upon a project they like, that decrease in traffic can make a big impact on your funding.

I was part of an anthology project to raise money for the medical bills (and burial expenses) of a fellow author which we had to do on Indiegogo because of Kickstarter's newly imposed ban on charities. The anthology included some mega-best-selling fantasy authors with huge followings. We met and exceeded our goal, but having just come off the triumphant run-up of *Athena's Daughters*, and having seen how many brand new people came into the project because of Kickstarter's massive exposure, it was pretty clear that the two sites are not equivalent. Kickstarter is like having a storefront in the Mall of America, and Indiegogo is like being in a plaza on a side street.

Another difference is that Kickstarter requires you to meet your base funding goal or forfeit all money earned, which is returned to the backers. Indiegogo gives project managers a choice on whether to set a campaign up to be all-or-nothing or to be able to keep whatever is earned, whether or not the base goal is met. Indiegogo and Kickstarter also differ in their fee for the use of the platform, among other differences. Make sure you understand the pros and cons of each site before you set up your campaign.

It may be that Indiegogo is pursuing more niche markets like start-up equity and fundraising to carve out a place for itself that is not in direct competition with Kickstarter. It's a fine site in many regards, but be aware of the differences between the sites when you have to choose where to crowdfund your project.

PATREON

Back in the Middle Ages, artists, authors, musicians, and performers like Michelangelo and Raphael had patrons, wealthy people who supported them so that they could make art. Sometimes the patrons paid for commissioned pieces showing a favorite scene or for a portrait. In other cases, a patron might underwrite a creator's living expenses to assure that the artist could focus on making art rather than be consumed by earning a living doing something unrelated.

Patreon brings the patronage system back in the same way Kickstarter democratized angel investing, creating a model where small payments by regular individuals underwrite projects the patrons want to see continue or expand.

Most people who set up a Patreon site are in a creative field: artists, authors, musicians, filmmakers, photographers, performers, inventors, and so on. In general, successful Patreon users have proven themselves and built a following outside of the site. It's not a place for first-timers with an unproven track record.

Patreon plays on the idea that hard-core fans will kick in a few bucks a month for special access to someone who creates what they enjoy consuming. They either make a one-time donation in exchange for a known reward, or more commonly, set a monthly subscription level that gets them a promised set of extras not available anywhere else.

For example, authors who use Patreon attract their "rabid" fans to become backers, in exchange for special content or engagement. Content rewards might include sharing deleted scenes, snippets of works-in-progress, holding contests to name characters, writing very short "drabbles" of story to satisfy patron prompts, or posting special patron-only video messages from the creator. Some creators offer patrons at certain funding levels early access to their newest work. Engagement might mean hosting a group Skype call at intervals, being online for a Q&A, and interacting with patrons in the special patron-only comment sections.

Patreon is an online VIP suite, the Internet's version of a private reception or box seats. Creators don't expect that their patrons are going to fully support them, but if they can gain enough reliable monthly contributions to pay a couple of monthly bills, it's a help in professions where cash flow is notoriously unstable. Patrons get special access and bragging rights, and the creator not only gains an income stream, but also the opportunity to nurture and engage with his or her most enthusiastic fans.

The model is set up for individuals, not companies. It's definitely built on the brand of a creator's name and reputation, and by building strong bonds with the most engaged segment of the artist's following, Patreon extends the creator's influence. Credibility is key, as with Kickstarter and GoFundMe. Crowdfunding models only work if the project owner delivers what is promised. Trust is the essential component, and that is built by reliability and keeping promises. Don't get into Patreon if you're not willing to deliver for the long haul.

GoFundMe

GoFundMe is the online equivalent of putting out a donation jar or holding a car wash to raise money for a cause. It's a crowdfunding Website designed for personal causes, not for business use. GoFundMe is a way to raise money to meet individual needs, like covering medical bills or college tuition, or to create a central donation point for a charity, nonprofit organization, or cause. Kickstarter does not permit fundraising, and Indiegogo spun off its fundraising elements to Generosity.com.

GoFundMe caters to individuals helping other people. Paying for medical bills is an all-too-common need, and GoFundMe makes it possible for far-flung friends, family, and supporters to contribute on a one-time or recurring basis. The site is also good for helping to deal with local, regional, and national natural disasters, gathering funds for supplies or equipment.

I'll talk more about crowdfunding, Internet fundraising, and charities in Chapter Sixteen.

THE LAST WORD

Crowdfunding can be an emotionally and financially rewarding effort with proper planning and hard work. These sites are still new, relatively speaking, so much of the territory is unmapped, waiting for innovators to see new and exciting ways to create campaigns and use these tools. Be sure you do your homework before launching a campaign, and make certain you have resources in place to handle fulfillment to keep backers happy.

NEXT STEPS

1. Explore Kickstarter and the other sites mentioned in this chapter. Get a feel for their capabilities and differences. Take a look at pricing/fees, terms, and overall feel.

2. Browse live and completed campaigns to see what others are doing. Look within your niche as well as at highly successful projects in other fields. Note how the projects are structured, watch the videos, and study the reward levels.

3. Back campaigns to get the true flavor of the sites (many projects have minimal levels at $1–$5). Pay attention to the communication you receive from the project managers. Do you feel cherished or forgotten? Are you "in the know" or digging for updates?

4. Kickstarter offers how-to guides, and there are a lot of specific resources available. Take advantage of these before you plan a campaign, and get to know people who have run campaigns to get insider tips.

Chapter Eleven

Social Amplification and Gamification

Now that you're putting out better content than ever before on social media to maximize your brand, influence, and credibility, you want to make sure it's seen by as many people as possible. Not only that, but wouldn't it be nice if people had fun engaging with your content, so much fun that it felt like play?

Those two elements—extending reach/visibility and making engagement fun—are at the heart of social amplification and gamification. Not surprisingly, the two often go together.

Social Amplification

Social amplification occurs when your content gets seen by a viewership larger than its original audience. It doesn't have to go "viral" as in crashing the Internet. As with audio amplification, there are levels. You start with a conversation among friends. Then you use a microphone to reach a larger group in a classroom. Next is a stage at an event, and then maybe an arena in front of a sold-out stadium. Translating that to social media terms, getting beyond your immediate circle of friends and followers is the first hurdle. Reaching the friends and followers of your core audience is the next level of influence, and then beyond that, two or more degrees of separation, to strangers who share common interests.

If you've seen "boosted posts" on Facebook and "promoted tweets" on Twitter, and their like on LinkedIn and other sites, you've seen one level of social amplification. These paid posts have a variety of targeting options. You can specify just your friends and followers (essentially paying to reach the people who have signed up because they want your content, which is somewhat held for ransom by the site's algorithm). You can also specify the friends and followers of your current contacts, or people "like" them in shared interests. Or you can enumerate the specific interests or behaviors of your ideal audience and let Facebook find them for you.

Anecdotal evidence and personal experience with Facebook suggests (although I can't prove it) that paying for amplification gradually yields diminishing returns. Initial boosts seem to reach a larger audience than do later ads, with the same budget and similar content. I'm not talking about click-throughs, which certainly can decrease as the newness wears off of an ad. I mean "reach"—the number of people who get to see the ad, something that should be possible to guarantee. It might have to do with a peculiarity of the algorithm, or maybe it's like any addiction—it takes more every time to get the same high. Buyer beware.

Twitter ads don't seem to suffer from the same attrition—at least, they don't yet. That might be a feature or a bug, and it may not last, but for now "promoted posts" with good content and good targeting deliver pretty consistent numbers.

Amplification offers two key benefits: reaching new people who have enough similar traits to your tribe to be good potential customers; and the possibility that a percentage of those people may not just buy your product, but also follow you on social media, thus increasing your organic reach and influence.

In addition to promoted content, a second form of social amplification occurs when you make your content available in places where others are encouraged to share it. Sites like Digg, StumbleUpon, and Reddit have taken the place of the office bulletin board, where people used to thumbtack interesting cartoons, articles, and bits of information. The whole purpose of these sites is to make good content more easily discoverable and shareable through crowdsourcing. In other words, everyone on the Internet now has access to tack up what catches their fancy on the big intangible bulletin board in the cloud. At one point or another, each of these sites has been hailed as the "front page" of the Internet, and there's a degree of truth to that, if (keeping to the newspaper analogy) everyone in town got to contribute and vote on what content went on the front page of the paper.

Rules vary by site. In some cases, it's okay to post a link to your own content so long as it is informational and not salesy. On other sites, the very act of posting our own link is considered overtly promotional and may draw ire. Read the rules and observe site etiquette. If you're not supposed to post your own links, hire someone to do it for you. If you can post for yourself, don't abuse the privilege and make sure the articles are truly content-rich.

A third level of amplification occurs on sites like Social Buzz Club. This paid membership site encourages users to share each other's content, making it easy to upload your own blogs and articles and make them available as tweets, Facebook posts, LinkedIn posts, and more. Because it's a membership site, there's a higher level of accountability to post good content. After all, it's pretty obvious if you're posting information no one else deems useful enough to share. Helpful, informative content gets rewarded by being shared more often, which increases the credibility and influence of the author.

As with the rest of social media, the premise of being a good neighbor and giving first will never steer you wrong. Go onto these sites with as much enthusiasm for finding great gems to share with your audience as you have for making your own wisdom easy for others to find and share. Be generous in sharing great content. Not only will that build trust with other site users, but your own followers on other social media sites will begin to see you as the helpful curator of good information, enhancing your credibility. Others may actually come asking for you to share their content, a measure of growing influence. The shift won't happen overnight, but if you're consistent about posting and sharing great information, it might occur sooner than you imagine.

SOCIAL GAMIFICATION

People are more likely to do something if it's fun. Why fight human nature? We all know what's "good for us," but we default to what we enjoy. What if what was good for you was also fun to do?

If you've ever entered an online poll, draw, or contest that collected your e-mail address or opinion, you've tasted gamification. It's so much more fun to type in social profiling information if the quiz promises to tell us which celebrity is our secret soul mate than it would be if the questions were asked outright. Participating in a poll or giving up our e-mail addresses for the chance to win a prize is more exciting than just filling out a form. Behind every one of those "games" is someone gathering a list or data mining.

Take a look at the online promotions and e-mail ads from major retailers, and you'll see an increasing trend toward gamification to encourage higher engagement. A really good "game" with a satisfying payoff (with or without monetary value) will get shared to a wider audience.

Gamification doesn't have to be complicated. Offering a random winner chosen for a prize from each month's new and existing e-mail newsletter subscribers is a type of game. Promising Facebook friends a free downloadable goodie if a post gets a certain number of shares is another easy game. The social excitement of Kickstarter has a lot in common with being at a racetrack, urging on your favorite horse.

Social Buzz Club is a social amplification site built around a gamification concept. Members sign up because they ultimately want other people to share their content, and are looking for good content to share on their own pages. The game comes in the process. Members have to share other content 10 times to earn enough points to be able to post one piece of their own content. This incentivizes and rewards the kind of behavior the site owners want while making it fun. The goal is to get members out of the rut of overpromoting and to grow their influence by sharing good content from other experts.

In addition to the main Website, Social Buzz Club also has a Facebook group where people connect, collaborate, and learn strategies for sharing influence. The group organizers bring in speakers, trainers, and experts to

SocialBuzzU.com and have created a value-added learning center for all Social Buzz Club members.

GISHWHES (the Greatest Internet Scavenger Hunt the World Has Ever Seen) is an example of gamification that straddles both the online and offline worlds. Virtual teams compete to complete lists of unusual tasks and upload photos and videos of their results. Tasks range from silly to difficult, from pure fun to performing random acts of kindness, and have succeeded on a large enough scale to earn seven spots in the *Guinness Book of World Records*. Winning teams get an exotic (and whimsical) trip with event founder, actor Misha Collins.

Sites like FreeRice.com, RecycleBank.com, and KahnAcademy.com are examples of gamification to encourage and modify behavior to reduce world hunger, increase recycling, and encourage learning. Recipe contests and bake-offs (which encourage the use and purchase of branded products) by food manufacturers are additional examples of gamification projects that have proven successful through time and exist both online and offline.

THE LAST WORD

Talking about your products and services to the same group of people has limited returns. Growing your audience requires expanding your reach. Social amplification and gamification can help you do that while creating a helpful and fun experience to engage friends and followers. No one said good content had to be boring!

NEXT STEPS

1. Take a look at the sites mentioned here. See what other experts in your niche are doing, and then look for best practices from successful people in other industries. Don't limit yourself to only use techniques within your field. If an approach works, borrow and adapt it.

2. When you're the consumer, be aware of invitations to gamified activities. How do retailers and other businesses dress up data collection or boost engagement with fun?

3. Think about how to make social amplification tools work for you to reach a broader audience. Make your content valuable enough that others can't wait to share it.

INTERVIEW WITH LAURA RUBINSTEIN

Laura Rubinstein is an award-winning social media and marketing strategist, best-selling author of *Social Media Myths BUSTED: The Small Business Guide To Online Revenue*, and cofounder of Social Buzz Club.

Q: How does Social Buzz Club work to amplify members' content and make the process fun?

A: Social Buzz Club emphasizes two elements: tribe marketing and gamification. It's designed to ensure reciprocity.

One of the problems for people starting Facebook groups is that they ask for shares, but the conversation becomes one-sided. With Social Buzz Club, members win and get options for increasing visibility by sharing other people's content.

When members share content and do other things on the site, they earn points. This reciprocal process brings out the best in people, and it's self-policing. People won't share poor content, so everyone is encouraged to up their game when they read the quality of others' content. Members increase traffic to their blogs because they are sharing content, and links to their blogs are being shared by the Social Buzz Club influencers.

People sharing your content is the highest compliment someone can give you on social media. Sharing encourages reciprocity even without the game. If you give, people naturally want to give back. Sharing encourages connection across many social media platforms and builds community.

Social media makes it easy to access people who want to be accessible. You can build your influence if you are passionate about your topic. If you want to amplify your social media voice, you need to find other influencers to help you. When influencers share other influencers' content, it builds everyone's influence.

For those who aren't yet celebrities, you can grow your influence by sharing the content of influential people.

Reciprocity is the cornerstone of the success of Social Buzz Club; it's all about building the tribe.

The first rule of networking is giving first. We make sure you do that; we invoke the law of reciprocity. It feels good to give.

People forget to post regularly. Social Buzz Club provides a way to make sure you have great content and keeps you top of mind in the home feed of LinkedIn. If you want to stay present and don't have the time to create your own content, curate the best of other people's content and you become a hero for your readers.

Social Buzz Club encourages users to embed video in their blog posts and then share the blog post. Social Buzz Club is a blog curation and sharing system.

When you reward good behavior, you increase connection, interaction, and engagement.

When you put a bunch of like-minded people together, they want to stay together and play together. Wherever I go, members of Social Buzz Club feel connected to other members. People love giving back.

Social Buzz Club has created increases in traffic of up to 1,600 percent for regular bloggers because it encourages shares, not just retweets. New shares equals new eyeballs equals more traffic equals higher search results.

Sharing blog posts is huge for SEO—it creates more "off-page" traffic sources, which leads to more insights on which network is responding. Sharing on multiple peoples' pages and at various times of the day cuts through clutter.

Klout/Kred/Alexa—if you put in tweets that mention your Twitter handle, you get more visibility and interaction. Sharing and being shared builds your score.

Q: Can you explain a little more about the idea of how gamification works?

A: Everyone wants to know what am I going to *give* out of this, not just get. That has been the secret sauce for Social Buzz Club's continued success. There's accountability to reciprocate through the gamification. Thus, you win when you give.

Reciprocity is the secret weapon for building visibility. Some sites do well with encouraging good behavior, but gamification is the best way to bring out the behavior you want. Reciprocity is naturally viral. We're seeing more gamified Websites for this reason.

Loyalty programs, rewards cards, and affiliate marketing—these have levels of gamification through the rewards.

Incentivize the right behavior without having the program get in the way. Done right, gamification becomes irresistible. It helps businesses and rewards consumers. When it's done right you create engagement, loyalty, conversion, referrals, and sales. Make it fun and grow sales.

— SECTION FOUR —

BEYOND THE BASICS

Chapter Twelve

Why You Still Need a Website and a Newsletter

Your Website is your permanent home on the Internet. As wonderful as it is to have a strong presence on social media sites and as gratifying as it might be to have thousands of friends and followers on Facebook and Twitter, your Website is your homestead on the electronic frontier.

Likewise, your newsletter subscriber list is an asset you own, unlike the friends and followers you amass on social media platforms. If Facebook or Twitter shut down tomorrow, you would have no way to reconnect with the people who have followed and liked you. But your permission-based opt-in e-mail list is one of your most valuable business assets.

Websites in a Social Media World

I talked earlier about the choice between having a traditional HTML-based Website that requires expert help to update and having a WordPress-based blog site that you can largely update yourself. That's an important choice, but equally important is what you make of your own little corner of the Internet with the content you share.

You may or may not sell products and services from your Website, but you most definitely are selling "you." Your Website should be the nexus of your brand, a place that builds, reinforces, and showcases your credibility, and a one-stop display of all you offer. If someone has heard your name and wants to know who you are, what you do, and what's so special about you, your Website should answer those questions and more in a compelling manner.

First things first. Choose the URL for your site carefully. Although options have broadened for the extension at the end of your URL (.com, .biz, .tv, .net, etc.), most people are used to typing in .com by default, so if you choose something else, you're likely to get some lost traffic and confusion. Try to buy the URL closest to your own name as well as the name of your company. That's easy if you've got an unusual name, and harder if you don't; but even if you have to use a middle initial, you really want to own your name online. (The same is true for your Twitter handle and other online sites, even if you don't intend to be active right away. Lock up your name before someone else grabs it.)

You can own multiple URLs and have them redirect to the same site. So you can have a main URL that is your name, plus URLs for your products, company, brand, signature event, and so on. Domain names are relatively cheap, so it's better to own ones that apply to your current and future products rather than put off securing them, only to find someone else has taken the ones you want.

Your landing page is the first page people see when they come to your site and when they follow or type in "YourWebName.com." Make it conversational and compelling. Video here is great, because it's like a warm personal welcome to your online home. Offer a gift for signing up to your e-newsletter. Make it clear what your brand is and what outcome you provide. Identify your target audience. Make it easy for people to realize they're in the right place.

Two important but underrated pages for your site are your "About Me" page and your "Contact Me" page. Your About Me page should be a quick recap of the experience, education, and achievements that prove your credibility, served up in a concise, conversational style. Don't make people search to find verification of your expert status. Your Contact Me page should give an e-mail address, phone number, and social media links to help people connect with you. I'm leery of just having an e-mail form for people to fill out. Many people balk at those form e-mails, and if your site isn't working well for some reason, you could be missing out on leads. If you provide an e-mail address, even as an alternate, people who really want to reach you have a way to do so.

Group your pages to make content easy to find. If you serve multiple audiences, group the related products and services by audience to direct users to the right set of items. Look for natural groupings such as "events," "products," "coaching services," "books," and so on. If you are selling from your Website, that entails a whole different level of expertise than we can delve into here, so be sure to work with a Web design professional who is experienced with e-commerce.

Likewise, "squeeze" pages (direct sales pages designed to provoke an emotional response and build tension culminating in a sale) are also a specialized art. A growing number of "squeeze page generator" software packages are available that help you create and customize templates from proven squeeze page designs. Some of these programs even work with WordPress.

YOUR NEWSLETTER LIST IS GOLD

There's a saying in the online world: "Your list is your retirement." This means that your opt-in, permission-based mailing list is an asset from which you can generate lifelong earnings if built well and handled correctly.

Although you own your URL, even Websites age and need to be replaced. But your mailing list is one thing which is 100 percent your own. Building a list comes down to two key elements: having an attractive incentive and having a good e-mail program.

An incentive is what gets people to hand over their e-mail address and give you permission to remain in touch with them. Just collecting e-mail addresses isn't enough; in fact, doing that without express permission to remain in contact can lead to hefty fines and big legal trouble. The CAN-SPAM Act is a law attempting to cut down on spam e-mail, and it requires that a user give permission before being added to a mailing list. (The Canadian and European laws about e-mail are even more stringent about privacy than U.S. law, so if you do business there, make sure you know the rules.)

How do you get permission? You tell people up front what they're agreeing to when they fill out an e-mail form. So whether you're offering a freebie, enrolling them in a program, signing them up for an event, having them respond to a poll, or drop their card in a fishbowl for a contest, make sure you clearly say that their e-mail address will be added to your mailing list. Let them know they can always unsubscribe at a later date. The "unsubscribe" language is important, because it's illegal to add someone and not make it possible for them to leave the list. Don't play games with the disclaimer. Make it very clear that to get what they want, they are agreeing to give you what you want.

Next up is a good e-mail program. There are plenty to choose from: AWeber, MailChimp, Constant Contact, and more. Programs vary in cost and services, but at the least good programs provide templates to make it easy to create a professional-looking newsletter, subscriber lists to manage your contacts, and metrics to measure effectiveness. You do not want to send out a newsletter to a slew of names typed into your Outlook e-mail. Not only is that unprofessional, it violates privacy laws and it can get you kicked off your Internet hosting servers.

If you want to go a step further, use an additional program like ConvertKit to create a sales funnel with autoresponders to make it easy to reward subscribers. "Autoresponders" are a sequence of preprogrammed e-mails that provide content to recipients during a set period of time. They're a set-it-and-forget-it way to offer something like a free download of a book or article in exchange for subscribing, and then follow up through the next few weeks with additional downloadable "thank you" gifts to rapidly build the like-know-trust element. You can use a program like ConvertKit to provide fulfillment and then export the subscriber e-mail addresses periodically and upload them to your main mailing program.

Make it easy for people to join your newsletter. Have a sign-up on every page of your Website, on your Facebook page, and on your blog. Use your event registration and event prize drawings to add to your list (with proper clear notice). Use gamification to make it fun. Use Rafflecopter to run contests that collect new e-mail names for your list. Do random drawings from new and long-time subscribers for prizes. Run polls on social media and do a random drawing from those who answer and provide an e-mail address.

Use your newsletter to give your readers useful content. That can mean repurposing articles or blog posts on your expert topics, sharing excerpts from your speeches or books, or sharing original musings designed to be of value to your audience. Tell them about upcoming events you're attending, share new products or services, and include new testimonials and event photos. Don't be afraid to share the spotlight. Add interest and value by highlighting news about colleagues that might be valuable to your readership. Generosity always pays dividends.

Consider cross-promoting with colleagues who offer products and services that complement but do not compete with your own. Host them for a guest article in your newsletter, and ask them to return the favor. You'll gain exposure to their list, and if your guest post includes an incentive for readers to subscribe to your newsletter, you might pick up some new people. Have a regular section in your newsletter where you give a shout-out to new products, books, and programs, and let the people you've highlighted know about it. One good turn deserves another!

Here's where you use the power of the social media echo chamber. Post a link to your newest newsletter edition on Facebook and Twitter, just like you do with your blog posts, and encourage your friends and followers to subscribe. Have links in your newsletter to your blog, Facebook, Twitter, and LinkedIn pages, and encourage subscribers to friend, like, and follow you. Separately, each venue is likely to miss some potential readers. Using them to echo each other, you're much more likely to reach a wider audience.

THE LAST WORD

Don't dismiss Websites and newsletters as obsolete! Look for ways to reinvent, refresh, and repurpose to bring new power to these tried-and-true means to stay connected and engaged while maximizing your brand, building your influence, and extending your credibility!

NEXT STEPS

1. Review your current e-newsletter. Make sure the layout looks modern and fresh, and check to assure that your unsubscribe notice is easy to find.

2. If you're not using an e-newsletter program, explore the options and look for one that not only fits your current needs, but has upgrades for additional services you can add as your business grows.

3. Read up on the CAN-SPAM Act so you understand e-mail best practices. If you work with customers in Canada or Europe, make sure you know what their laws require.

4. Think about what content you can reuse and repurpose for interesting newsletter articles. What incentives can you offer to attract sign-ups? How can you incorporate a request for sign-ups into your ongoing social media, presentations, and events?

CHAPTER THIRTEEN

SOCIAL MEDIA, BRANDING, AND INFLUENCE

Remember that old song "Every Breath You Take" by The Police with the recurring lyric about watching someone? Hum it to yourself every time you're on social media as a reminder that you're in a fishbowl.

Financier Warren Buffet said, "It takes twenty years to build a reputation, and five minutes to ruin it." On social media, that has narrowed to five seconds. One moment of frustration or anger can go viral, reaching the world with no do-overs. It used to be that a momentary lapse, a joke told and later regretted, and a word spoken privately in anger might be forgiven or discreetly not spoken of to others. As we live out our lives increasingly on camera and captured by social media (our own and that of others), that grace period is gone.

Your brand, reputation, and influence are both powerful and fragile. Powerful, because built right and handled carefully, they can be your legacy, outliving you and changing the world one life at a time. Fragile, because one lapse, one misstep by you or your designated people can ruin what you've built in ways impossible to fix.

BRANDING

Your brand is a combination of tangible and intangible factors, all of which you can control to some degree (and some of which, admittedly, you can't). Tangible branding includes your logo, tag line, product design, packaging, delivery method (in some cases), and pricing. Intangible branding includes the promise you implicitly make to your customers about the outcome your product will achieve for them, your reputation, customer satisfaction levels, market positioning, and what your brand represents in the world.

Some brands represent luxury and implicitly promise wealth, sexual attractiveness, fame, and power (think of high-end automobiles, jewelry, and watches). Others reinforce the idea of home, family, friendship, community, nostalgia, and warm memories (Coca-Cola and Subaru excel at this positioning). Still others promise good times with friends and family (beer, restaurants, resort destinations). Then there are brands that take a stand on an issue, like Tom's Shoes (each purchase triggers a donation that provides shoes and other services in poverty-stricken areas), making their activism an integral part of their brand.

Every action you take online and offline either strengthens or weakens your brand. Do your best to assure that everything you post and tweet reinforces the image you want the world to have of you and your brand. Recognize that you *are* your brand. That doesn't come with an "off" switch. It's a 24/7 responsibility.

If you act in alignment with your branding and provide added proof that what you offer is legitimate, your credibility grows. But if your actions seem out of sync with—or worse, contradict—your branding, customers will react negatively, and the damage to your brand can be deep and long-lasting.

In today's social media fishbowl, branding extends past the product to the distributors/customer-facing staff and those running the company. Get caught saying something derogatory or unkind, and you'll see your mistake go viral, costing you customers. At best, your PR people will have to do damage control. At worst, a portion of customers will not believe your apologies and take business elsewhere.

The easiest way around this is to try to be a sincerely nice person. If you can't do that, keep a lid on your less respectable impulses, and realize that someone always has a cell phone to pick up photos, audio, and video.

REPUTATION

Both you and your company/product have a reputation. When both are in sync, life is good. When there's a disconnect, problems happen.

Word of mouth has always been crucial to building and maintaining—and ruining—a reputation. In the old days, whispers and rumors got passed from one social circle to another. Now, thanks to the Internet and social media, those rumors reach the world in seconds.

Sites like Yelp, Angie's List, Travelocity, Google Reviews, and Amazon make it easy for customers to share their experiences with products and services. Most shoppers report being at least a little bit influenced by online reviews and many turn first to customer comments before buying. People who are angry are more likely to want to tell the world than people who are happy, meaning that you'll have to work to encourage satisfied customers to post to sites while upset clients are already motivated.

Good service and a good product matter, but mistakes still happen. When they do, how you respond can make or break your reputation. Be transparent, be responsive and polite, and be visible. Engage with the person making the complaint politely and get the details. Do everything you can to make it right. When you respond like this in a public forum, you can sway the opinions of onlookers even if the original customer remains angry despite your efforts. Sincere efforts to fix a problem and take care of a customer count for a lot, and many people are willing to give the benefit of the doubt when they see proper recourse being taken.

Don't stonewall or get into an argument. Don't get hung up on trying to prove who is right or wrong. Don't lie or threaten. These actions will poison your reputation and alienate bystanders who are following the online conversation. The Internet never forgets. Even if you win the argument, you lose.

Your personal reputation hinges not only on what you say and do, but what kind of content you create, what type of content you share, and whose information you find worthy of sharing, as well as where you go, how you treat people, and the causes you support (both with the company and as an individual). There are no secrets anymore.

Some people recognize this and choose to be neutral in their presence, so as not to offend anyone. Others make their opinions and causes known and embrace it as part of their brand, recognizing that it may cost them some customers. Only you know which of those options is best for you, but what you do or don't do should be part of a conscious choice and not haphazard. People respect consistency, even if they don't agree with your stand.

INFLUENCE

Influence flows from your brand, reputation, actions, and connections. Influence is the weight your opinion holds to be able to sway the actions or opinions of others, as well as your ability to tap into a network of people who are willing to help you make something happen.

Your influence grows in direct relation to your ability to be of service to other people, to help them accomplish their goals. That's why growing a large social media following, amassing a large newsletter subscriber base, gathering sizeable crowds at your events, or selling a lot of product matters. All of those elements provide you visibility and a voice whereby you can give a signal boost to other people and causes. Influence starts with what you can do for others, and pays you back in reciprocity.

Reciprocity is a key element of gaining and using influence, and in social media, it's easier than ever before. If someone posts a great review or writes a nice article about you or your company, use social media to tweet the link and thank them (thus gaining them increased visibility and potential new followers). Retweet, like, comment, and share when someone mentions you, therefore giving them a social thank-you that further raises their signal. Proactively boost the signal of people you admire in your industry—thought leaders, successful entrepreneurs, speakers, authors— by sharing and commenting on their links. Whenever you can connect people who share a common interest or mission, make the effort.

At the same time, pay attention to who understands the influence game. People who only take and never reciprocate run into problems. Look for good partners by seeing who thanks and acknowledges those who provide help. Those people are likely to make the best collaborative partners.

THE LAST WORD

Branding, reputation, and influence are intrinsically interconnected. Damage to any one piece ripples through the others. Strive first to earn and maintain an excellent reputation, and carry that into the branding for your product. Then give first when you connect with others and build your influence, which in turn burnishes your reputation and your branding.

NEXT STEPS

1. Google yourself and see what comes up. Then take a look at the ratings that affect your business (Amazon, Yelp, etc.). Resist the temptation to ignore negatives without giving them serious thought. Are there ways you can improve performance? Are there areas in which you excel that you aren't making the most of for your brand?

2. Think about your branding. Is it current? Does it reflect where you are and where you're going? Is it too limiting or too vague?

3. Take a look at your sphere of influence, both in person and through sites like LinkedIn. How could you expand your reach? How can you warm up or strengthen your connections to the people you already know?

INTERVIEW WITH STEVE OLSHER

Steve Olsher is the *New York Times* best-selling author of *What Is Your WHAT? Discover The ONE Amazing Thing You Were Born To Do* and cofounder of Push Button Influence.

Q: Where do social media and influence intersect?

A: Social media has dramatically changed global accessibility. Our society has embraced living vicariously through others and not only condones this practice; it is encouraged amongst virtually all subsets of our population. More so than any other time in the history of mankind, we have an unprecedented level of societal data and information insight. We are now able to be the ubiquitous fly on the wall. In a sense, it's societally acceptable voyeurism with willing participants on both sides of the glass.

Whether you like what you see or not, you are influenced by the stimulus you encounter. When one puts something forth for the world to judge, the public acts as both judge and jury and chooses to accept or reject what's presented. And, when a post is created, no matter how innocuous, others' lives are influenced. For better or worse, this is our new societal norm. Reality dictates that not all posts are created equal. Some go viral, some won't. Why do certain anomalies achieve the rare state of viralocity? Because, they typically show effort, are inspirational, educational, or controversial. And, without a shadow of a doubt, the majority of the time, it's just dumb luck.

Historically, viral content is tied to outrage or unique, singular entertainment. Ultimately, mindless content such as Grumpy Cat is the lowest, yet simplest, form of entertainment to create. And, given that most people need a break from reality, it resonates with people from all walks of life.

We have accessibility and connectivity through myriad social channels that total in the *billions* of daily active users with endless terabytes of user-generated content being created by the minute. When, since the dawn of man, has one person been able to connect with so many simply by pushing a button?

What we're witnessing is unprecedented. The sheer mass of the number of people online is staggering—and the access they grant into their lives via these social media channels gives every Dick and Jane the opportunity to impact millions across the globe. The nature of celebrity has changed as we have ostensibly assassinated the gatekeepers. Back when there were limited information/content distribution networks and decision-makers, a *very* limited number of people were granted the keys to the celebrity kingdom. Today, the power of creating mass visibility lies in the hands of the masses. Inevitably, this translates to a substantial increase in the odds of different types of talent from all walks of life being discovered. The pure definition of what lies unabated within the "public eye" has been dismantled.

How one approaches influence should largely be dictated by their overriding career objectives. More often than not, significant influence is a direct reflection of having one area of focus that is interchangeable with what someone is known for. The more one can hone in on a specific area of expertise, the easier it will be for *their* people to find them. In my *New York Times* best-seller, *What Is Your WHAT?* the focus is on identifying one's core gift, the vehicle they'll use to share that gift, and the people they're most compelled to serve. Answer those questions and you hold the prescription for influential success.

Ultimately, the key is being different from others—which simply translates to honoring how one is naturally wired to excel. Find your voice by honing in on what resonates deepest. On the business front, companies that struggle do so because they lack clarity on their unique value proposition. They have no identifiable voice or personality and, therefore, fail to connect on more than just a surface level with consumers. If one is going to start a business, for all that is holy, create something that stirs not only the soul of the people they serve but, also, its founders.

Q: How does video factor into the influence game? Is it now as important to look good on video as it is to have real expertise?

A: Video is, bar-none, the most intimate medium. Without exception, everyone who wants to dance in the influence space will eventually embrace video and the future of interaction is surreal. For example, if one conducts coaching services, virtual reality based coaching realized through near proximity technologies, will allow the coach and client to, for all intents and purposes, be sitting right next to each other, regardless of locale.

Let's be honest, not everyone is "glamorous" and, fortunately, it doesn't matter. To find success in this evolving landscape, glamour is *not* a prerequisite. One simply needs to convey their abilities to help those who can benefit from their expertise. The old mechanisms of transmission are dying off, so there's a risk if the shift to video is not embraced. Anyone can broadcast their brilliance and knowledge and this, in and of itself, is attractive. So, no, you don't need to be a star or gorgeous to find success with the medium. People will resonate with the message and the messenger. Glamour alone is not a sustainable character trait.

Those who are most successful using video leverage the medium by focusing on a specific area of expertise. The greater the degree of knowledge and ability to teach, the greater one's visibility will inevitably become and, potentially, their ability to be "found." At the end of the day, it boils down to expertise and enthusiasm. The more one has of each, the larger the tribe will be that they subsequently foster.

More and more people will shift toward video as their favored new media platform. Though it seems like a far-fetched statement, video is still in its embryonic stages when compared to other "old school" media. Newspapers have been around for hundreds of years. YouTube only came into its own by 2006. As a general whole, there has yet to be mass acceptance of video as a primary marketing tool. We have a long way to go until we've achieved widespread adoption.

Q: What do you think is most important for maximizing brand, influence, and credibility?

A: The process begins with identifying your topic of influence [TOI]. A lot of people don't have that nailed down. Without the TOI, it's nearly impossible to gain traction and momentum. Once your TOI is established, the next step is to choose the preferred broadcast platform—audio (recorded or live), video (recorded or live), blogging, social media, or mobile. And, a strong online focus combined with offline initiatives such as speaking, teaching, or networking is an unbeatable strategy.

In Push Button Influence, we strongly suggest implementing the M3 Process—modeling, marketing, and then, monetizing. Too many aspiring influencers attempt to bypass this proven framework. This is not recommended. Find people who are where you want to be, model their tactics and strategies and then, and only then, should one shift to focusing on marketing which leads to the Holy Grail, monetization.

INTERVIEW WITH TERESA DE GROSBOIS

Teresa de Grosbois is an international speaker, trainer, and four-time international number-one best-selling author and author of *Mass Influence: The Habits of the Highly Influential*. Teresa also heads The Evolutionary Business Council, a community of emerging thought leaders who focus on teaching the principles of success and prosperity.

Q: You've written about how influence is acquired and used. Where does social media come into the picture?

A: The biggest thing to understand is that social media is not to sell you. Social media is like the apple pie you bring to meet your new neighbor to build a relationship. Use social media to endorse and praise others, and your own influence will grow.

Think about who you can shine a spotlight on. Keep your focus on others and it comes back to you.

Understand that you can't make yourself famous. You need other influential people to talk about you. So talk about them. It used to be that to become highly influential, you had to be talked about in the media. Now it happens on social media.

I spend two minutes every morning acknowledging and shouting out people who have made helpful contributions. Start doing that, and you'll be surprised where you are in a month. For example, doing a #FF (Friday Follow) on Twitter is your way of saying "these are great people to follow." Little acts and gestures count. Retweets, photos taken when you get together with people, all build energy.

Gather like-minded individuals who "get it"—the more you pass the puck, the more people want to play with you. Help those like-minded individuals, and they'll help you in return.

Video gets content out fast. It's a great opportunity to get together with people you admire and interview them, get them to give testimonials. Create awesome content and give influence to others.

Use the natural ratios of giving more than you ask. So, do 10 posts about something useful to one post about you selling.

Gamification works best when you combine social media strategy with what you're doing live, so combine live events with social media. For example, giving your room a hashtag to tweet out photos and play on the big screen in the room gets everyone in the room having fun and tweeting about the event.

Social media is one form of communication, and power increases exponentially when it is blended with real life.

Q: In your research, what have you identified as key habits of influential people?

A: Play big; be of high service to others. Find out what problem you solve for others. Stand apart and invent new possibilities.

Be authentic. Authenticity is when your inside voice is saying the same thing as your outside voice. You're authentic when what you're saying and doing and thinking are all in alignment.

Be in a one-to-many conversation instead of a one-to-one conversation. Social media is a one-to-many conversation, but it can also be a many-to-many conversation. Influence increases when people see you as a content expert. Some social media, like your Facebook page, Facebook Groups, LinkedIn Groups, or Blog Talk Radio are one-to-many conversations.

Influence is the currency of the influential. To build relationships with influential people, offer to help them increase their influence. Get them a speaking gig; shout out their content on social media. Social media helps us to build our relationships with influencers by offering to increase their reach (influence).

Understand that the most influential people become a hub for others in their field. They help the influencers in their own field. This is true of some of the most successful Facebook groups; they share posts by other people.

Where you can create a hub/tool for influential people to use, you expand your own influence. The Evolutionary Business Council created a Meetup group; now it's one of the biggest groups in Calgary and the idea has spread to other cities. Every individual brings some of their influence to the group, and the influence of the group as a whole grows faster than any one person, spreading the energy out.

Influence is a lot like a sport. Some people never pass the ball back, then the team stops passing the ball to them. Passing the ball is not a burden. Giving influence to others is similar. It becomes natural and intuitive to give and return influence to others. Your own influence builds as you give influence to others.

Chapter Fourteen

Go Global, Stay Local

Whether your company is purely local or has a global footprint, you need to be active and visible on social media. Why? Because your prospects and customers expect you to be findable online, and will consider your absence to be suspicious, perhaps even unprofessional.

When a potential new customer meets you, he or she is likely to look for your Website to verify the first impression and gather new information. Depending on your type of business, someone might turn next to LinkedIn for a look at your profile, connections, recommendations, and endorsements, as well as your resume. Or, they might look at Angie's List, Yelp, Google, or Amazon to see how your product or service ranks and what customers say. They might check your blog to see your articles, videos, photos, and event updates. Odds are good they'll look for your Facebook page and Twitter feed to see what kind of recent news, specials, coupons, or details you've shared, or to get a better sense of your personality.

Any time you leave a void in that cycle of discovery by your absence, there's a piece missing in the puzzle. Your prospect is trying to put the pieces together to get a complete picture of who you are, how well you serve your customers, how you see your role in the world, and how much you interact and engage with others. If you're not findable on social media with recently and consistently updated content, you risk looking unapproachable at best and behind the times at worst.

STAY LOCAL

I've heard owners of mom-and-pop local businesses ask why they need to be on social media that is seen around the world when their customers come from down the street. There's a curious perspective there, assuming that only people in far-away places use the Internet. The short answer is because your local customers also use Facebook.

Social media has become the source for news and information for a large (and growing) chunk of the population, across all age and economic brackets. Smartphones and Wi-Fi have helped to put the power of a computer and the connectivity of the Internet in reach of most consumers. So it's natural that people turn first to social media and mobile apps to decide what to do next weekend, where to go for dinner tonight, what movie to see, or what the flavor of the day is at the local ice cream shop.

Consumers make purchase decisions based on the information they find online. If you're a restaurant without a menu online or without a way to share daily specials, some customers will go to a competitor where they can be sure to get what they want. If you're a nightspot without a way to advertise the featured drink-of-the-day and tonight's live music, you'll see business go elsewhere rather than show up and be disappointed.

Even if you're not in a retail or hospitality business, you probably aren't the only business in your field. It's a definite disadvantage when your customers can learn more about a competitor with a few Web clicks than they can about you. Highly motivated prospects may make the effort, but most won't bother. Now that people are used to being able to do some "stealth" intelligence gathering by going online, it seems intrusive and bothersome to make a phone call or request information by mail. And if your business is clinging to antiquated delivery systems, prospects may wonder if you're mired in outdated ideas in other areas.

Consider your social media sites to be ways to show your engagement with and participation in your local community. Do you support local school or community sports teams? Show pictures from the games, show off the jerseys your company underwrote, and celebrate the team's victories and trophies. Do your employees volunteer locally? Post pictures from your latest project, whether it's putting in flowers at a local school, building a Habitat for Humanity house, or helping with a holiday toy drive. In fact, you can use the power of the Internet and social media to encourage more people to donate or volunteer for the local causes you support, and to provide recognition and acknowledgment for those who do.

Don't be afraid to have fun. Use the gamification principle to run online contests, or ask your followers for their opinions with polls. Polling is fun and social when you share the aggregated (anonymous) results because everyone wants to know what other people think. Polls can be serious (like having people pick their top concern about retirement), or fun (like picking next week's featured flavor), or whimsical (like naming a company mascot or a lawn decoration or even a large piece of equipment).

Remember that social media is supposed to be social. Use it to get into conversations with your most enthusiastic customers. Find out what else they like aside from your products to flesh out a psychographic profile of your core tribe. You might get great ideas for collaborations, joint ventures, or cross-promotions. Ask their opinion, even if it's about who might win the Super Bowl or what the best green bean casserole recipe for Thanksgiving is. People love to be asked, and they love to share. Give them glimpses of your life outside of work: pets, hobbies, vacation snippets, favorite foods, etc. In a world where people feel increasingly disconnected from others, sharing personal touches builds community and also strengthens the like-know-trust factor.

As a local business, your localness is one of your greatest strengths. Play up your participation in local festivals, parades, sporting events, school programs, street fairs, business organizations, charities, and recreation. Snap pictures of you and your employees out and about in local places or nearby parks or attractions. If you are the most recent proprietor in a long-running family business, then share old photos and reminiscences. Give shout-outs to customers who get recognized for being active in local community-building, charity, business, and education programs.

If your company provides a scholarship, then make an event out of it, naming a recipient and posting photos.

Find ways to celebrate your locality on social media and make your online pages a go-to place for your customers and neighbors to find out what's going on, see their friends in action, and be seen interacting in the community. Your Facebook, Twitter, Pinterest, and other sites can become the online equivalent of the neighborhood's favorite front porch, where everyone gathers because that's the place to find your friends.

Go Global

Even if your clientele spans the globe, you can use many of the engagement strategies outlined in the Stay Local section, just tweaked for your broader market. Instead of focusing intensely on one location, emphasize the worldwide nature of your work with travel photos, pictures posted by your customers from various countries, or quizzes and contests with a globe-trotting focus.

Use case studies and stories to illustrate how your services or products make your customers' lives better in all the global marketplaces you serve. Demonstrate your adaptability to differing cultures while emphasizing the common successes and outcomes achieved regardless of location. Play up your community and volunteer involvement regardless of where in the world your staff is located.

Though Facebook, Twitter, LinkedIn, and YouTube serve a global audience, it's worthwhile to look at which other social media platforms are popular in the countries where you have clients. Recognize that other countries may have different social norms about informality or sharing personal information in a business setting, so adjust accordingly.

Use Facebook and LinkedIn groups to build an online community of your raving fans. Give customers the sense of your personal presence with video, even if you're thousands of miles away. If there's a language difference, consider having subtitles in the native language if you're recording in English, or providing a translated text.

THE POWER OF COMMUNITY

Whether your business is local or global, creating a sense of community among your clients, prospects, and fans can be the glue that increases engagement and customer loyalty. Online communities often center on Facebook or LinkedIn groups, which have replaced more cumbersome group-management software programs.

One of your first questions will be whether to make the group public or private. If your first priority is to gather new members of your tribe and bring them closer into your orbit, then a public group is the place to start. You can invite people to join the group as your "ask" in your videos and social media messages. The group is also a natural follow-up for people who have attended one of your events or Webinars and want to discuss what they've learned. You can reward members with additional free content to draw them further down your sales funnel, providing e-books, short videos, checklists, articles, and worksheets. Plan to be present some of the time, but also build in ways to encourage your members to keep the conversation going and support one another.

If you are looking to strengthen the bond among your inner circle of fans or dedicated customers, or if you plan to use the group as a way to share paid content, then the group should be private. Many people create multiple Facebook groups, one of each of their signature courses, seminars, or events so that attendees can bask in the afterglow, engage with each other and with the presenter, and receive additional VIP content for which they have paid an extra fee.

If you need more features than just an online place to meet and have ongoing conversations, you may want to step up to software that will let you create a members-only forum with additional features such as calendars, polls, and tools to make the site easier to moderate. Some options include MyBB, which is free and open-sourced, and BBPress, which was developed by the WordPress people and integrates easily with WordPress blogs. Another system that has been around for a while and offers a wide array of features is Ning. Ning was one of the original do-it-yourself online community building sites, and it has a lot to offer, but not everyone will find it intuitive to use.

Meetup, which I talked about in an earlier chapter, focuses primarily on live events. But it does have scheduling and announcement, e-mail, and comment capabilities, and could be used in connection with an online venue for a public community that is looking to boost membership. Or you could add an online group component to augment a Meetup group's live events for additional or extended engagement and conversation.

Whether you are local or global, the goal of engaging customers and prospects on social media is to create a sense of community to build loyalty and help clients get the most successful outcomes from your products and services. Easy to use, affordable tools make it simple to build live or online gathering places to extend your brand, and influence depends on your goals. How much those gathering spots become actual communities depends on your intent, and in your personal investment of your presence and content.

THE LAST WORD

Die-hard fans and loyal consumers want to belong to communities of like-minded people. When you become the hub for a community that extends your concepts while engaging your followers, you extend your credibility and influence.

NEXT STEPS

1. If you belong to member organizations or the private or public groups of other subject matter experts, take a look at the sites with an eye toward layout, structure, extra amenities, and participation. Read the rules and gauge the quality of participation. How well does the group deliver on its potential?

2. Think about the strategies in the chapter about connecting your business to its local or global physical community. What activities are you already doing that might tie in with this? What new activities might be easy to add or extend?

3. If you're considering starting an online community, think about the pros and cons of public vs. private, and determine how the community fits into your overall strategy. Administering or moderating a site and providing your personal presence, as well as generating content, requires a sizeable and ongoing commitment. Determine how interested you are and whether or not you can allot extra resources to help.

INTERVIEW WITH GAIL WATSON

Gail Watson cofounded Women Speakers Association in 2011, committed to a vision of a world in which women are empowered to authentically express themselves; to build a thriving, prosperous business; and to feel a part of something greater.

Q: What does it mean to build a community of interest in the age of social media?

A: It's all about building networks. The strategies are similar to list-building, but the Internet accelerates the effort. Building a community offline takes time because it's all face-to-face, people need to physically attend events, and you build your list and invite them. The Internet uses the same strategies in a better use of time. You can reach more people in less time without physical travel.

It's the same principles to build online as offline. When you meet people, get their e-mail address and permission to contact them. Keep them updated; own your list. The number one way to reach your database is still through e-mail.

In the online world, an engagement strategy is critical. This is where communities fail. Don't engage in long conversations if you mean to meet and connect. For Facebook groups, don't add people to the group without permission. That makes people shut down, out-and-out, block you, and you lose contact. Make them want to join. E-mail lists must also be opt-in.

Set a strong intention for the group and grow organically. Grow slowly and work out your systems. Set rules and guidelines in place to know how you're going to act and interact on the group and enforce them. Groups need good management.

Women Speaker Association's Facebook group is a place for discussion and sharing experiences and resources. Not for self-promotion. We curate to assure members adhere to the guidelines, or we remove them. We don't allow disruption.

Building an online community takes one to three years. It takes about three business quarters to build live events and a lot of up-front work. You spend a lot of time on engagement. We led both live monthly events and online events. People take their cues from how the leader engages. Community liaisons get people talking and keep the conversation going. The members do introductions and approach wallflowers, so no one gets left out and everyone feels welcome.

Too many communities rely on technology and not on personal engagement. Building that is up to you. It doesn't happen overnight. You slowly see the build online and it's really exciting. An active community has people commenting on posts, liking, and sharing. The group must build trust, and that happens by enforcing the rules, monitoring activity, stepping in when needed.

The line between online and live begins to blur. People love videos on Instagram and Facebook; 50-second blurbs are really popular. They get to see your face. It's almost like a live connection.

When you engage in the online world, it's easy to post, but we need to remember there is a real live person on another screen somewhere who wants to see your face. If we don't respect that, you'll lose them. They want to get to know you and be with other people, connect with others, especially when they work from home.

You need a personal touch. People miss that in the online world. We do all our calls via Skype or Zoom and use video. People want to see you, look into your eyes, and get your body language. Personal interaction really solidifies the connection. We immediately invite new members to weekly live video events, group chats, one-to-ones, education that is not just a recording.

Our number-one strategy is that we must get e-mail addresses in order to be able to invite people and keep in touch. We don't own the social media platforms. They could stop at any time or change the rules, just like Blab just disappeared.

We will never be held hostage by a social media platform again. We lost our content on Blab and had to move our community to

Zoom. But now we created SpeakerSuccess TV, so we record our Zoom events and post them on the new Website. That way we keep the content, people can interact live or see past replays, and we can also prerecord. Blab shutting down turned into a gift, because we learned not to be dependent on a social media platform.

Social media platforms are great for list building. Remember that "free marketing" costs you time. You own the e-mail database; it's your number one asset. It affects your reach and attractiveness for sponsorships. When you own your database, you're not dependent on platforms. You can still contact people. Facebook generates 80 percent of our new contacts.

You've got to stay on top of new technology and apps and share them. That's how you become a community of value. Don't keep secrets when you find something new and cool. Share what works and what doesn't work.

INTERVIEW WITH JO DIBBLEE

Jo Dibblee is a social entrepreneur who sees it as her responsibility to give back, both locally and globally. The founder of Frock Off Inc., Jo is described as a tenacious and fearless philanthropist—a catalyst to change. She is an international award-winning author, event leader, speaker, and the author of *Frock-off: Living Undisguised*, which stems from living in hiding for 35 years as a key witness in a murder investigation.

Q: Creating community is very important to you with Frock Off Inc. What have you learned about building live and online communities?

A: The critical question for those we attract, especially in all the noise, is "what's in it for them?" In this noisy and hectic time, standing out means providing value—serving.

The great thing about Facebook is it doesn't matter where I am. We can be having a heart-to-heart conversation regardless of geography.

We build community in so many ways. We can reach out to anyone anywhere, and this applies in particular to the now widespread use of video. Social media plays such a pervasive and pivotal role in society today. It's not only in our lives, but as an entrepreneur, it plays a significant role in our business—it touches every area of our life—making it easy to share pieces of your life and your day, allowing others to get to know more about you.

Social media allowed us to reach out to everyone and build community, to be authentic in a way that serves the audience. Social media engages and creates awareness. There is a critical intersection of social media and live events. When attendees can participate and communicate before a live event with others attending through social media, barriers are removed. Allowing access, connection, and possible collaboration even before you walk into the room creates a level of familiarity. It helps to set the stage for expectations. We've already broken through the barriers of people needing to warm up because of Facebook, Twitter, and LinkedIn.

Because of social media, people are ready to participate fully in the event before it begins, allowing them the opportunity to maximize their return and set expectations. Further social media allows event producers to showcase and shine the spotlight on attendees—an added value.

Even at a large event, the group feeds its mindset in advance on Facebook by getting excited. We eliminate that initial awkwardness, and we can talk about the transformation they can expect. Social media also sets the stage for accountability. We use this to pave the way for our attendees to ensure the maximum return. It's not just pumping them up with motivational hype; participants who are engaged gain a glimpse of what to expect. The pre-event work sets them up for success—to determine any gaps in their life or business. Further, they are well aware of their "ask" once the work is complete.

Engaging with the audience via social media before an event allows us to serve them at the highest level. Also, it acts as a self-selecting system for those who are not prepared to do the work. They'll vet me out, or I'll vet them in if they're right for the event. Even before our guests arrive, they have a clear understanding of what to expect, allowing us to ensure delivery of our promise.

Q: **You make a concerted effort to stay continually engaged with your audience. How does that work?**

A: We use LinkedIn and Twitter to support Facebook. We stay connected in between events. Time differences and distance don't matter. Social media is convenient, and it's easy to stay connected and current.

After each live event, we maintain an ongoing event Facebook page where we post inspirational tidbits, and reminders of their role and their accountability. We celebrate and share wins as well. It's easier and more cost-effective than the old way, but more so, it's social and creates a stronger community.

Caution: if you're using Facebook only for promotion, it won't work nor will it keep people engaged between events.

If you're using social media for business, be careful what you post; be careful how you show up. Watch out for negativity. You don't want to create a negative after you've made an initially positive impression.

We don't just say "see you next month." Our members keep the conversation going continually, and it's not just the leader of the troops. We encourage our members to support each other. How you show up matters. We tell them to think about what they want people to know about them from how and what they share on social media.

Social media is one of the most cost-effective ways to launch your business and brand. We are always testing interest with questions, or posting something funny to make people laugh. Social media has changed how attendees and members relate to each other. Like attracts like. When social media is strategic and thoughtfully delivered, it attracts and allows us to be transparent and approachable—real! People want real substance and engagement.

Attendees are now savvier. They expect and want more—much more—than hype and so they should. If people aren't authentic, it will come back to haunt them. You must be in alignment with your business message. When I consider attending an event, my litmus test is: does this opportunity meet my mission?

Don't try to do too many things. Be careful that anything you promote is in alignment. Be consistent and strategic, not a one-hit wonder and then MIA until the event; you won't get the engagement you need, and participants will be less likely to refer or return. Be out on social media three to four times a day. I'm regular enough with my posts that people notice if I slip up. Don't post personal dirty laundry or bad days. Look for the happiness factor. Don't post when you have a chip on your shoulder, or you're on edge or angry.

Reframe challenges to focus on the silver lining. If you have a public profile, people will find you. Don't burn bridges. Negativity attracts negativity. Don't use social media to vent. People feel anonymous on social media, but they're not.

You have a responsibility to your online community to show up in a way that serves others. Leave people in a better place than where you found them.

Don't get addicted to having people validate your comments on social media and tell you how wonderful you are. If all you're doing is trying to get your cup filled, you're not real. It must be about the service you provide, not the validation you're getting.

I live my life full on and am living the life I talk about—I am transparent. Sharing my story is intense. Initially, I worried about serving my audience or opening up wounds that I was not equipped to address. I didn't want to do any further damage to anyone. But I wanted them to see what's on the other side of trauma.

Today, I often find myself feeling gobsmacked about what is going on in my life. I love sharing the excitement of the journey I'm taking with others. The support is mutual and creates ripples of change. If you're not prepared to do what you say, don't put it online. We have a chance to show up as what we preach. I want to see you do what you say, not just talk about it. Social media has raised the bar on expectations, so people are seeking those who are real and helps them to see through false claims.

INTERVIEW WITH KATANA ABBOTT

Katana Abbott, CFP, is a life and legacy wealth coach and the founder of Smart Women's Coaching. Katana is also the founder of Smart Women's Empowerment, a nonprofit online resource center focused on helping women unlock their financial power, where she hosts *Smart Women Talk Radio* with more than one million subscribers. She is the author of several books, and the founder of The Designated Daughter Caregiver Program.

Q: What have you learned after a decade of creating online communities?

A: I started Smart Women's Coaching in 2006 with an online audio course and survey. There were very few financial empowerment programs on the Internet at that time, and we offered live calls, created our Idea Lab, and explored what we could do. I built a strong community and a team of experts who shared knowledge with the community, with each other, and cross-promoted. I tried to do it live and local, but we didn't have the critical mass. However, the right people started to show up when I created the online community. We grew to a membership of 300. This was before Facebook, and it required some complicated software called iGroops. Now, everyone uses Facebook or LinkedIn groups.

Today, I focus on private coaching, speaking, teaching, and the radio show. Several years ago, I transitioned the Smart Women community into a nonprofit called Smart Women's

Empowerment (SWE). Many of the people in the community couldn't afford private coaching, and many were going into debt trying to learn how to start a business, so I decided to provide free financial education to women around the world who could access the Internet. I hadn't realized that creating the community as a nonprofit was originally an option, and if I'd known, I would have done it that way from the start.

I aligned with an existing nonprofit organization to create SWE as one of their projects. We now offer the radio show, expert blogs, and a new video course with cutting-edge content. The program is free to the public because it is funded by donations, grants, and sponsors.

Originally, I had a Website and list built by live events and an e-mail newsletter. We then created Smart Women's Café, an online community. I looked for strategic alliances with other organizations before social media took off.

When I started the Internet radio show in 2008, we created Facebook and Twitter sites for the show to promote it and created a system to automate a weekly newsletter as we built a following. My assistant promotes the show before it airs, does live tweets and Facebook posts during the show, and helps guests promote with prewritten tweets.

Smart Women's Empowerment is a Website. We also have a Facebook page for *Smart Women Talk Radio*, and I've got a Facebook group for my private coaching clients called Midlife Millionaires. The new course, Unlock Your Financial Power, will be free, online/Web-based, with video, audio, text, exercises, and contributing experts who provide content and refer to resources. We may add a Facebook group and live Q&A calls.

I blog each week, plus there's a weekly newsletter with my personal message where I promote what is going on both locally (where I live) and in the online community. I post it as a blog, and it auto-populates to Facebook and Twitter. Facebook is a long-term big commitment because it must be managed regularly. The contributing experts' blogs are also included in the newsletter with links that go to social media and our nonprofit Website.

My listeners and clients are from all over the world. We are in the process of shifting from live radio to podcasting. We have one million subscribers to the podcast and have done over 300 live episodes. Now we're going to prerecord and go to a 15- to 30-minute format with very targeted content.

With radio, the real growth is in podcasting. People tend to listen outside of drive time. They like to listen when it fits their schedule, and live radio doesn't do that. My audience follows me on social media, and we created a mobile app for Smart Women's Empowerment that collects all our blogs and radio show recordings and creates a push notice when there is new content. We offer listeners the flexibility to join us on-demand. There is so much content being consumed.

Chapter Fifteen

Social Media Tips and Tricks for Authors, Speakers, Event Planners, and Content Creators

Authors, speakers, event planners, and other artists/creators are especially poised to benefit from social media's power, both for its ability to promote and to connect in ways uniquely suited to the demands and challenges of these particular professions.

Social media works especially well for this group of business owners in five key ways: branding, influence, credibility, connection, and engagement. Let's look at their common social media needs and then take a look at more specific recommendations for each group.

Branding: Authors (whether of fiction or nonfiction), speakers, event planners, and creators are a brand in themselves to an even greater degree than other professionals because their whole product relies on their own intrinsic talent and personality. Many books have been written and many speeches have been given on every topic, but a new best-seller becomes a hit because of the author's unique perspective and voice. A stellar event takes on the personality of the long-time planner/promoter. Creative professionals, whether they are artists, musicians, game designers, etc., dare to bring something they have created into the world that is one-of-a-kind because of their insights and past experience.

It's important to realize that your brand is not the title of your book, your series, your speech/event, or the name of your product. There will be many books, series, speeches, events, and products—all tied together because you created them. *You* are the essential common branding element. Understanding this from the beginning makes your online life much easier. Get your name as a URL and either make it your main Website or have it redirect to your core site. Use your name for your Facebook fan page, Twitter feed, and YouTube channel. That way you don't have to start from scratch every time you bring out a new book or product, and your audience will accumulate in one place, instead of being fragmented across many smaller sites. That makes updating and maintenance much simpler and keeps it easier to remain a consistent presence.

The only exception is if you have an "alter ego" creating a completely different type of book, event, or product with a totally different audience. For example, I also write fiction (epic and urban fantasy) for several large publishers. Although I'm open about this and view it as an essential part of my differentiation and branding (that is, transformational storytelling in a marketing setting), I have separate Websites, Twitter, and Facebook pages for fiction and nonfiction because the interests and audiences are too divergent. Some people follow both "sides" of me, but most are only interested in one or the other, so mixing the information (beyond what I talk about on my personal page on Facebook where I'm mostly just me) would be too confusing.

Influence: Authors, speakers, event coordinators, and creators rely heavily on their personal networks. Some of this is due to the nature of the work, which tends to be largely individual, thus creating the need to tap into the outside grapevine and personal connections to get news, discover resources, and gain recommendations that lead to new projects. As content and artistic creators, your work revolves around telling stories and truths, often with a goal of personal transformation. That requires a high level of personal influence, in order for your content to be heard and received.

This makes it particularly important to remember that every action on social media affects your connections with other people and, thus, your influence. Your livelihood relies on you nurturing and expanding your personal connections, so every interaction should enhance and not detract. Not only should you consider your social media posts from the standpoint of reinforcing your brand, but you should also communicate with a plan to strengthen and expand your influence, especially because publishing, professional speaking, art, and events tend to have a very small, tight-knit constituency.

Credibility: As with branding, your livelihood as a subject matter expert and purveyor of wisdom depends on people believing that you are who you say you are and that you know what you claim to know. Without that, you have no platform. Make sure that all of your social media posts enhance your credibility, because the only thing you are really selling is you. Consistency between your image and the reality of who you are is essential to your credibility, and to maintaining charismatic integrity.

Connection: On one hand, writing, speaking, event planning, and creating seem very public, because your work gets put on display for the world to see, often to large audiences at once. Yet there's a lot of behind-the-scenes solitude that goes into crafting a book or speech, putting together an event, or making art. Social media is an easy and effective way to stay connected to your fans in between new releases and events. In today's world, you can't afford to be absent for the months or years it takes to create a new book, piece of art, composition, or event. People have short memories, and there's a lot of noise coming from up-and-coming players. Use your social media channels to keep your fans informed about what you're doing, what's happening next (and when), and where to find you.

Engagement: Connecting with existing fans is one important use for social media, but so is building engagement with current and prospective fans. Utilize the "social" part of social media to ask questions, have conversations, and find out what your audience most wants to learn. Encourage feedback on your books, art, events, and speeches to discover how to serve their needs even better. They will love being asked and feeling that they play a part in determining what you bring to market. Engagement also creates a stronger tie between you and your audience than you gain from just informing them of coming attractions.

Facebook, Twitter, and LinkedIn are the three vital core sites for speakers, authors, creators, and event coordinators. I'll talk about more specific social media in a little bit, but when you're just getting started online or if you can only maintain a vibrant presence in a few places, start with these three. These sites are essential because they reach the largest audiences, are the first place others will go to check you out, and help you make the broadest range of connections. Use Facebook and Twitter to stay connected and engaged with your fans and prospects. Use LinkedIn to nurture connections with your fellow professionals, vendors, resources, mentors, and other experts.

Your blog is also an essential part of your social media success if you're an author, speaker, creator, or event runner. All the things I mentioned earlier about blogs holds true, with the additional caveat that your personal voice matters even more. You can use your blog to delve into the story behind your books, speeches, and events. People love to see "behind the curtain" and get the origin story for your characters or concepts. You can also react to news stories or current events that have some connection to your story, speech, or event and share your personal take on the situation, revealing glimpses of how you think and how you view the world. Let your readers see a little of who you are outside of your books and presentations. Most importantly, get a conversation going and keep readers connected and engaged.

Before we move on, I want to touch on one more common aspect, and that's "charismatic integrity," which I mentioned earlier in the book in the interview with Michael Port.

Remember when I said that your personality and perspective makes your books, speeches, events, and art unique no matter how many others have addressed the topic? Part of that uniqueness comes from your one-of-a-kind perspective, your singular journey to overcome and learn in order to reach the conclusions or insights you share in your work. But another element comes from your charisma, that indefinable "something" that attracts certain people—your tribe—to you.

Some people are blessed with an innate ability to turn the world on with a smile and attract people to them almost from the day they are born. Others grow into a more nuanced charisma, born of experiences, mistakes, hard-won truths, and self-knowledge earned from pain and effort. It's a little like the difference between someone who is beautiful like a classic sculpture, and someone whose face testifies to character. Both are attractive, but whereas one is effortless and an accident of birth, the other is the result of triumphing over life's ups and downs.

Charisma can be innate, but it can also be developed. It can spark an immediate attraction, or come from multiple exposures and be an acquired taste. One thing that holds true, however, is that people who are passionate about their message and comfortable in their own skin, without pretense or manipulation, exude a natural charisma that stands the test of time.

The other piece of "charismatic integrity" is "integrity." That's different from "credibility." Both credibility and integrity rely on trust, but where credibility has to do with having a true, believable message, integrity means that you are who you say you are, across every situation.

We've all either had or heard about experiences where a personal encounter with a celebrity or hero has turned out badly. Maybe the idol turned out to be self-absorbed, too busy, or downright rude. In the worst cases, the icon turns out to be nothing like his or her image. If the celebrity is an author, speaker, event emcee, or artist, the truthfulness—credibility—of the work is not affected. But the integrity of the creator takes a damaging blow because the image is a sham. When integrity is violated, the credibility of the work rarely continues to matter. Violating integrity breaks the like-know-trust contract so profoundly that the audience no longer wants to hear the message from the messenger. And in a world were social media, cell phone cameras, and Wi-Fi means perpetual scrutiny, a bad experience with a single person can destroy a career that took decades to build.

Social Media Tips for Authors

In addition to the core sites I talked about earlier in the book and in this chapter, there are some important social media sites just for authors and readers, and some ways to use previously mentioned sites that apply especially to authors. Let's explore them and see how to get the most out of your time and energy.

Amazon offers a free "author page" for authors whose books are for sale through the site. Look for "Author Central" and follow the instructions to set up your page with your photo, biography, video, and social media links. Your Amazon author page will show up whenever the site serves up a list of your books. You can even connect your blog so that every time you post to your blog, your author page gets an updated link/ synopsis. Not only is your page a one-stop place for people to find out more about you and find all your publications, but anyone who "follows" your page will get automatic notifications whenever you add a new book.

Author Central is free, and in addition to your author page, signing up also gives you access to some of Book Scan's reports to help you track your sales. Although self-published authors can easily look directly at their sales numbers, authors who rely on a traditional publisher only receive reports twice a year. Being able to check your sales in between reports, or whenever you run a promotion, can be very helpful.

Goodreads is another essential author site. Though Goodreads is designed more for readers than for authors, it is a vibrant—and huge—community of people who love books. Like any community, Goodreads has its own norms and etiquette. Please take the time to read the instructions for authors and follow the guidelines. Goodreads readers are extremely welcoming for authors who take the time to approach them correctly, but things can get prickly if you go charging in with a heavy self-promotion vibe.

Sign up for an author page on Goodreads, and you've got your own bit of online real estate in a vibrant hub of authors and readers. Make sure you've got a good photo and bio, and then link your book videos, blog, and Twitter account (another place your posts will automatically update) and make sure all your books are showing up in the list of your works. If something's missing, it's easy to link the absent book so that it does show up. Goodreads' "librarians" are very helpful in a pinch, but the instructions are good enough that you won't need much help.

Explore your new page. You can list upcoming events, like book signings and author appearances, and make yourself available to take questions from interested readers. Goodreads encourages its members to read and review, and many Goodreads reviewers cross-post to Amazon. As a reader yourself, you can upload the covers of books you've read to your digital "shelf" by using the helpful mobile app to scan the book bar code, thus sharing your reading list with your fans and friends.

Goodreads also makes it very easy to invite your Facebook friends to join you on Goodreads. You'll want to do that because the environment to discuss books is much different—and dedicated—on Goodreads than it is on Facebook. Check out the many groups on Goodreads dedicated to different books or genres, and consider starting your own group. Unless you're already famous or the book is a big best-seller, you might want to start out creating a group on a topic instead of just about your own books (check existing groups so you don't duplicate). You can always create a group about your book(s) later.

Goodreads giveaways are a great way to whip up some excitement about your new book and get it into the hands of people who are likely to read and review. You can also use the "events" function to create online chats scheduled in advance to connect with far-flung readers who can't make it to a live event.

Relate to members as a reader first and an author second on Goodreads and you'll build good relationships. Recommend books you've enjoyed by other authors, but remember that publishing is a very small world, so if you post reviews, only post positive comments. Negative posts are very likely to reach the author, whom you might find yourself sitting next to at an event in the near future!

Pinterest can be another good site for authors, if you use a little imagination. Start with "pinning" (adding photos) of your book covers. Then create boards related to the topics and themes of your books. That might include travel destinations and locales where the books are set, motivational quotations, photos of items mentioned in the books (for example, I have a whole collection of pictures of abandoned buildings on Pinterest that ties in to one of my fiction series), recipes, clothing, or lifestyle items. Or, make collections of things that interest you and share as a way to give readers a glimpse of the "you" behind the book. When you travel or attend events related to your books, snap photos and share them on Pinterest, Instagram, Tumblr, and Facebook.

NetGalley is a site providing free digital review copies of your book to bloggers and book reviewers. It is much easier (and less expensive) to share an e-book than to package and mail dozens of physical review copies. You can restrict who can sign up for galleys (which are often early uncorrected PDFs rather than final e-books) if you're worried about losing sales, but it's wise to err on the side of wider distribution to get more early buzz.

NetGalley reviewers can leave reviews on the site, but many also review the books on Amazon and on their own blogs.

Social media for authors also involves connecting with others in the publishing world, learning from other writers, and getting tips from those with more experience. A wealth of writing blogs exist to provide a wide range of information for authors on all aspects of publishing and the writing life, but one of the most established is Absolute Write, which bills itself as the "water cooler" for authors, just like the place conversation occurs in an office break room.

I've talked extensively about Kickstarter and Patreon in earlier chapters, and they're important sites for writers. Many authors participate in Kickstarter-driven anthologies, and established writers can use Kickstarter to underwrite new books in a series that's been cut loose from a publisher. Likewise, Patreon can strengthen your engagement to your core, loyal fans by providing extra content and additional access to you, the writer, in exchange for a monthly subscription fee. Explore what other authors are doing, and see how those sites might fit into your promotional plans.

Revisit the chapter on e-mail newsletters, and take the advice to heart. Building your newsletter subscriber list gives you direct access to your most engaged fans. Use a mail program that includes landing pages and autoresponders, or utilize an extra site like ConvertKit or BookFunnel to offer prospective readers a free story or book in exchange for signing up. I use Constant Contact's "event" software to create online promotions where I offer a free extra story or novella in exchange for sign-up with proof of purchase of one of my books. It's a great way to expand the subscriber list while rewarding new fans.

Let readers know where you're going to be by creating a list of upcoming events (signings, author appearances, book-related speaking engagements and events) on your Web page and in Goodreads. Goodreads even has a feature that will let subscribers know about author events in their ZIP code! Remember to mention events on Facebook, Twitter, and LinkedIn, and live tweet/post from events whenever possible.

Just because you deal with words doesn't stop you from using video. YouTube, Google Hangouts, Facebook Live, Periscope, Snapchat, and other programs can be great ways to liven up your blog and social media posts with a personal touch and let your readers feel like they've met you.

Do a video snippet from a book signing or author event, visit a site you've mentioned in one of your books and show your readers around, or just welcome readers into your workspace for a minute or two for a "behind-the-curtain" look at the writing life.

MAKING THE MOST OF SOCIAL MEDIA FOR SPEAKERS AND EVENT PROMOTERS

ESpeakers is a great site for speakers who want to have their sizzle reels seen by event runners and event coordinators who want to find new speakers. Make sure to fill out your profile fully, and take advantage of the options provided to help you find and reach your ideal audience. Several membership levels are available with varying services, but at the upper end, ESpeakers integrates with several major CRM systems, has tools for lead tracking and e-mail marketing, generates detailed reports, and has a mobile app. Beginning speakers will find the basic level robust and easy to upgrade. Take advantage of how easy ESpeakers makes it to upload video and connect to your social media networks, as well as its integration with speakers bureaus.

For finding smaller groups close to home or in specific cities, take a look at Meetup. I covered the general capabilities of the site earlier in the book, but I want to talk specifically about its appeal to speakers and meeting professionals here. Meetup makes it easy for event runners to gather an audience for one-time or recurring events. It's perfect for pulling together events for a tour, or organizing an ongoing meeting for a group or organization. And for speakers, it's a fantastic way to discover new groups that might be open to having you present to their group.

LinkedIn ranks up there with ESpeakers and a good CRM system for being a necessity of the speaking business. Add the casual connections you make to your friends on Facebook and Twitter, and invite the most valuable new acquaintances to LinkedIn. Share video snippets on your LinkedIn feed, and post a backstory about your topics and speeches in articles and blog posts, which you share on LinkedIn. Encourage your hosts and attendees to recommend and endorse you for your subject matter and speaking skills.

How long has it been since you updated your profile on NSA (National Speakers Association) or other speaking industry or professional associations in which you're a member? Life gets busy, and before you know it, your profile might be a year or more out of date. Sometimes, it's the simplest things that pack a lot of bang for the buck. Keep your profile and bio updated, add some fresh video snippets and video testimonials from recent events, make sure that your topics and events are current, and get a new headshot. If the sites have an online forum, be visibly helpful by answering questions, referring resources, and being of service, keeping your own profile high without being self-promotional.

If you're a speaker with a back of the room book, then everything I said earlier about authors also applies to you—with the addition that every opportunity to promote your book also promotes your events and vice versa. YouTube, Periscope, Facebook Live, Google Hangouts, and all the other easy video sites should be part of your everyday marketing arsenal. Take fans on tour with you when you travel, such as checking in from airports, staying at hotels, visiting event sites, and any extra sightseeing. Do one-minute interviews with other speakers and event attendees. Tell viewers how they'll get more out of the event by reading your book, or encourage people who have read your book to delve deeper by attending upcoming events. You can even have someone in the audience stream you on Facebook Live during a live presentation (if the event is free and open to the public).

If you're a speaker or an event runner, your permission-based mailing list is your lifeblood, and live or online events provide the perfect way to grow your subscriber base (just make sure people know you're adding them to the mailing list when they sign up for events, drawings, or information). Hold business card drawings at your events for prizes, or post an offer on your Website and blog providing a series of short video tips or an article in exchange for signing up with an e-mail address. If you're speaking at an event that you're not hosting (and therefore don't have access to the attendee mailing list), create a special offer (like a bonus Webinar or video series extending the event topic) that requires attendees to provide you with their e-mail addresses, and ask the event runner to share your offer with all the registrants. Put your newsletter signup or special offer link in every book and handout. Use Rafflecopter to manage online contests and capture e-mail addresses.

Your e-mail newsletter software should be robust enough to have services to help you grow your attendee base. Look for the ability to do online and e-mail polls to increase engagement. (You can also offer a freebie in gratitude to those who participate in a poll and share their e-mail address, which goes into your newsletter list.) Some programs, such as Constant Contact, have an event invitation component that is easy to use and includes a lot of useful options such as landing pages, autoresponders, the ability to accept fees and donations, sell product, and more.

Utilize Web video such as WebinarJam, GoToWebinar, and even Google Hangouts and live streaming on YouTube to hold your own online seminars. All-in-one programs such as StealthSeminar can handle live Webinars and automated replays with a lot of nice extra features. Webinars can be great ways to bring prospects down your sales funnel, lead people from your presentation to your book or coaching programs, or gather e-mail addresses. Best of all, you don't have to leave home!

NEW IDEAS FOR CREATORS ON SOCIAL MEDIA

Whether you're an artist, musician, filmmaker, designer, photographer, crafter, or other creative professional, you're looking for ways to grow your audience and share/sell what you create. Many online sales sites have social media components that can be helpful for connecting with customers and other creators, but you have to realize the potential.

Etsy is a core site for selling handmade, unique, or vintage items and craft supplies, and it also has a forum for discussion threads that you can use to connect and engage with shoppers. Etsy Teams is an online way to have conversations with customers and other sellers about the kind of items you make and sell. Etsy Local enables customers to find their favorite online Etsy sellers at live events such as craft fairs and street markets. Not surprisingly, Etsy makes it very easy to promote your items and Etsy page through social media on Facebook, Twitter, and other sites.

EBay isn't just the world's biggest yard sale anymore. If you sell through eBay, consider using its social media features to create "Collections"—themed groupings of items that you offer for sale to encourage customers to buy related and complementary items. Sharing your listings on sites such as Facebook is easy through the built-in interface.

DeviantArt is a well-established and popular site for graphic and visual artists that considers itself a community as much as a sales site. Profile pages, journals (in-site blogs), and folders (collections of items) make the site highly customizable for sellers and fans. Forums, chat rooms, and in-site e-mail (notes) enable and encourage conversation between and among artists and fans.

BandCamp, Behance, Musical.ly, and Dribble are other sites designed for connecting creative professionals with fans and customers. Look for ways to raise your visibility within the sites you choose so that you become part of the community and develop relationships both with customers and fans as well as other creators. Take advantage of the ability to share your posts on Facebook, Twitter, Instagram, Tumblr, and Pinterest with links back to where people can buy what they see. Use your blog and social media posts to share the story behind your work, your creative process, and even glimpses of works in progress to capture fans' attention.

Don't overlook the possibilities of YouTube, Periscope, Facebook Live, and so on to build engagement. Take your fans on location to street fairs, flea markets, craft fairs, galleries—wherever you show and sell your work. Upload short videos of you working on a new project, or talk about how you work and how you developed your unique style or technique. Do a one-minute retrospective of past pieces, or show "coming attractions" of new work. Team up with friends in the creative community to create videos that showcase several artists at once—perhaps combining music, performance art, and visual art. Bring your visual art to life with a "music video" and camera movement (look for royalty-free music from sites like MusicBakery).

Your e-mail newsletter list is just as important to your livelihood as it is for authors, speakers, and event runners. By building and engaging your subscribers, you can drive traffic to live events where you are showing or selling, to online sales and promotions, and to your own site to showcase your newest work. Reward subscribers periodically with digital bonuses such as sketches or single songs. Build your list by asking people to sign up when they browse your real or online booth. Advertise seasonal sales, holiday offers, or coupons, and take advantage of the connection between your e-mail newsletter software and social media sites to share your updates and encourage more people to subscribe. Use Rafflecopter to gather e-mails with online contests. Have a sign-up on your blog, Website, and on your Facebook business page. Let your online customers know that their purchases get them a free digital bonus and a subscription to your newsletter.

Patreon is perfect for creative professionals, and as you build a loyal and active core following, this site can help you reward them with unique digital content as well as additional access to you, the creator. Not only that, but Patreon is designed to provide an additional stream of income from subscribers that grows with your following.

If you need ideas for what to share with your Patreon subscribers, go see what other creators are doing and choose the best ideas to make uniquely your own. Sketches, glimpses of works in progress, subscriber-only updates on projects underway and upcoming, video clips, advance access to new products, and even podcasts are all popular content to share with your Patreon fans. If time permits, you may even want to offer some subscriber-only content to make the subscription worth their investment.

Kickstarter can be a godsend for creators—if you can inspire confidence that you will fulfill the project with a quality product. For this reason, it's good to have a track record before venturing into Kickstarter so that backers can feel confident that you will deliver the goods. Musicians, filmmakers, craftspeople, artists, and other creative professionals have used Kickstarter and crowdfunding successfully to bring specialty projects to life or get enough of a guaranteed preorder to make production worthwhile. A successful Kickstarter also creates a backer list, which can be invited to join your newsletter to get regular, non-Kickstarter updates on all your work.

THE LAST WORD

Social media provides valuable ways for authors, speakers, event runners, and creators to connect with your audiences and collaborate with peers. You can showcase your work and build your brand while demonstrating your credibility and extending your influence by being a good neighbor in these important online communities.

NEXT STEPS

1. Check out the sites I've mentioned and see what others are doing. What ideas do you get on ways you could use them to grow your audience?

2. Create a strategy before you sign up and start posting. Think about who you want to reach and what message you want to send.

3. Engage strategically and consistently to build relationships. Invite fans and friends from other sites to strengthen your bond and show them more about what you do.

4. Guard your brand and credibility by always posting and behaving with integrity.

INTERVIEW WITH BRYAN THOMAS SCHMIDT

Bryan Thomas Schmidt's books and anthologies have been released by Baen Books, St. Martin's Press, Fairwood Press, Titan Books, WordFire Press, and more. Novels Bryan has edited included *The Martian* by *New York Times* best-seller Andy Weir (Crown, 2014).

Q: How has social media affected publishing?

A: You have to have a social media presence to get anything going. Publishers expect you to be active there even before they give you a contract. It's part of the publishing marketing strategy. The expectation is that you will participate. Social media is especially important for small presses, because it's a playing field where they can do marketing on par with big publishers.

Social media has shaped reader expectations. Readers absolutely assume that they will interact with authors. They want it. You have to build relationships. It's all about getting to know the author personally.

Publishers have downsized their marketing departments. Their internal staff do many more jobs and multiple books are the responsibility of one staffer. Social media helps because it's free. It's easier to find and build relationships with reviewers on social media and it costs less than other types of marketing.

Social media is crucial to networking. I met a Titan Books' editor through social media and went on to successfully pitch books to him.

Blogging is important. Have a regular day of the week to post, and update regularly. Consistency is important. People need to know when to go to your blog.

Facebook for me is huge. I like Facebook better than Twitter because it's easier to have private conversations. Facebook chat is indispensable to me. I do a lot of book deals through Facebook chat.

Have an author (fan) page on Facebook as well as a personal page. You need to know what kind of separation between your personal and professional lives works for you for your health and safety. Use the security controls on Facebook, and decide how much you're going to talk about your spouse, kids, etc.

Podcasting is a great resource for writers. It's a useful tool. People like to hear your voice and inflection when you read.

Twitter moves so fast that you need to prepare questions for interviews—that makes it easier to be spontaneous.

It's easy for people to misinterpret on social media because they don't hear the nuance in your voice. It's good to be a guest on podcasts if you don't want to host or produce. Always look for new outlets, and be willing to talk about more than just the new book. What really gets people interested is being helpful, offering something to the community that they can use to improve themselves, their work, etc., from humorous banter to practical tips.

Q: You edited *The Martian*, which became first a best-selling novel and, later, a hit movie. Yet it all started online. Can you please share that story?

A: I met Jennifer Brozek through social media and we worked on one book together. Her old classmate Andy Weir asked her to edit his new book, but she felt she was too close to him. She sent Andy to me. That's how I ended up editing one of the early versions of the book.

The Martian was originally posted online. Andy got feedback on the science to make revisions, and his readers urged him to release it in e-book or print for sale. Andy came to me to help him clean it up for a final version suitable to sell. Later, an agent and editor found it and offered him the publishing deal.

Q: What are your thoughts on Kickstarter for authors?

A: Kickstarter isn't a good way to fund a novel from a writer who isn't already an established author. There is no way for backers to assure good work. It's great for collections/anthologies. You need to hire the right people to do a professional video and professional-quality book design. A Kickstarter campaign can consume 3–4 months before and 2–3 months after the actual campaign, so it's like a full-time job.

Hire an editor who is well-known—it adds credibility to your Kickstarter project.

Kickstarter comes with a risk. Supporters are outspoken and the platform tracks failure. People want to be part of a winning project, and the audience can be demanding.

Q: How has social media changed the publishing industry?

A: Authors who have come into the business in the last 10–15 years are more willing to promote their work. Older authors often resist that, but I have found it has become expected of you as part of a contract these days all too often.

Publishing has a core community, which is all the more reason not to be a jerk. Everyone talks to everyone. It's a small group that's active in the community. If things go wrong, word spreads and that closes future opportunities.

If you want to be an author and you haven't sold anything yet, it's the perfect time to get out here and build a platform. Don't wait until you've sold your book. Build your platform now for the book that will come out two years from now. Create relationships, build an audience, and build friendships with readers. It's not an instant leap and you're off. Preplanning is essential for blog tours. Be proactive, plan ahead a few months, remind people, and follow through.

INTERVIEW WITH RICK GUALTIERI

Best-selling indie author Rick Gualtieri is best known for his Bill the Vampire series of novels and his role as part of the Authors and Dragons podcast.

Q: How has publishing changed?

A: The changes in publishing put people just one step removed from the content creator thanks to the Internet. Now readers can post something directly to the author and get a response. That's not always a good thing, mind you.

These days, when someone reads a book and enjoys it, they can send a message, and the expectation is that they will be able to do so. It's to the author's detriment if he or she has no social media presence. Readers discover that authors are just normal people, and that's great. The "con" is that there is a dark side. A lot of creeps are out there. Being on social media opens you up to the awesomeness of people and to the ugliness as well.

Smart authors build relationships, and create a real presence with Facebook and Twitter.

Engage in conversation with readers, discuss theories about the books, and encourage reader interaction. You've got to know yourself. Some people should not be on social media if they're abrasive, don't know when to keep their mouth shut, or can't censor themselves.

Social media has given small and medium-sized publishing houses a bigger voice. It's a great equalizer for the small guys. The big guys (publishers) haven't quite figured it out yet.

Any new writer who thinks he or she is just going to write books and that's all has a wake-up call coming. You've got to discover your voice and boundaries. Global platforms give you a far reach if you learn to work it correctly, connect with people around the globe. Social media is a commitment. You can't give it all to an assistant. You can't take yourself out of it.

Don't make your books a secret, but don't shove them down someone's throat.

Q: What are your thoughts about Kickstarter and Patreon?

A: It's a mistake if you're just starting out, not sure what you'd be offering people. If you have a platform already, use Kickstarter to finish a series or start something new.

If the authors are willing to work on providing value, work your ass off to provide content, treat patrons really well, and give back, it can work. It's only hat-in-hand if you're asking something for nothing. You've got to hit your deadlines, reward patrons, and treat them well.

Q: Any advice for authors using Facebook, Amazon, and Twitter?

A: Post when you have something to say. Try not to put up too many posts. Say something at least once a day. Respond to questions and meaningful comments.

Getting in early helped. I beat the rush of authors (on Facebook ads). Once it gets crowded, it doesn't work as well. Everything changes. The ads that ran a year ago don't work now. Now I'm doing Amazon ads and I'm mostly on KDP Select and Kindle Unlimited. Be flexible, try new things; don't think you can set it and forget it.

For a lot of authors, Twitter is useless and becomes spam. The majority of any successful marketing lies in doing your own thing and standing out. Be a real person, have fun, and have real conversations. Try to be more interesting. Talk about stuff that you find interesting or stupid. Spend a couple of minutes each day on social media.

Be reasonable (on Amazon). Be a real person. Use keywords, but don't stuff your headlines. Read the rules. Act right away if you get a warning on a book. Never cause a bad experience for your readers.

It's an evolution. Look at what your competition is doing. I'm constantly learning about things like keywords, how to write a better book description. When things are working for you, don't make changes until they're not working as well anymore.

INTERVIEW WITH GAIL WATSON

Q: What should speakers know about social media?

A: If you want to stay in touch with your audience and create a following, speakers can interact more pre- and post-event through social media and video. Interact more, connect in masterminds.

Social media has huge benefit for speakers. Today's speakers engage more on social media, unlike the "fan clubs" that followed a previous generation of speakers.

Gone are the days when you are untouchable. People want to reach out and touch you. I have seen established speakers who don't engage. They are either superstars or their following starts to dwindle.

If you're not staying in touch with your fan base, they go elsewhere. They want real people, real stories, and interactions.

Someone said: are you speaking with your ego or our soul? Stay grounded with your "why." Why is getting it out to create change in the world. Stay attached to your why. Be happy to engage.

Don't worry that sharing content on social media is going to cannibalize live events or programs. Your knowledge and experience are not easily exhausted. Information is so accessible now. We want to know and examine your key points for WIIFM [what's in it for me?] and see your testimonials, what others say about you.

LinkedIn has easy formatting to ask for testimonials—so much reciprocity there. Copy and paste the testimonials you get on LinkedIn to Facebook, your Website, Instagram, etc.

Let social media tell a story for you from day 1. People want to check you out on social media and see how you interact. They piece together who you are. Don't consider your social media sites to be "yours." They are a billboard, an ongoing commercial of who you are. You want to organically attract people into your world. Be consistent with your message. It's a goldmine. Win people over with your commitment.

Video provides high free exposure. Just get out there and be the real authentic you. It doesn't have to be studio-grade video. A TV show reached out to Jo Dibblee because of her social media videos. People share your video on their timelines and it creates buzz.

Audiences today would rather have a real person being themselves. Oprah's fan base dropped when she lost weight because she wasn't as relatable. You don't have to be perfect/pretty or a TV model to do video.

The speaking industry has changed. Audiences are more savvy now. They want value, not just a good show. It's no longer about the table rush. They want real people and want to see how you are providing service.

I debriefed a very successful speaker once who asked me, "Did you like the tears on that point, or should it be before or after?"

It was a performance. It was fake. When it comes to my business and my life, I don't want to be fake. It's never a wrong decision when it's made out of love. Speak from your heart. Give a real message. People won't hear the stutters. They will hear your truth. People will feel your realness. That's your connection.

You don't have to be super-emotional or an entertainer. That's like watching a movie. If you intend people to act on your information, it doesn't have to be entertainment. You want them to learn and implement. The audience needs balance. Entertainment is okay, but you also want serious information. All kinds of speakers are needed. Know yourself and be true to yourself.

Chapter Sixteen

Not-for-Profit and Cause-Focused Grass Roots Social Media

Not-for-profit and cause-focused groups of all sizes are discovering that social media opens up opportunities to expand their donor and volunteer base while also engaging and educating the community and prospective clients about their services and outcomes.

We've seen the dramatic stories about microfundraising on Twitter after tsunamis or natural disasters, and bigger projects on GoFundMe or other crowdfunding sites. If you've been on Twitter, Pinterest, or Facebook for any length of time, you've probably seen pictures of cute, adoptable dogs and cats from rescue organizations and shelters all over the country.

These are just a few of the ways cause-centric organizations are reaching out successfully, and it's time your group got on board.

Social media is a natural outreach for cause-centric organizations because it's where the people are. Direct mail is expensive, and though it can still be effective, printing, postage, and handling costs can be daunting. Many modern donors look askance at "free" calendars received through the mail or slick, heart-tugging direct mail letters, because they know the costs of engaging a direct mail copywriter and producing giveaways eat away at any donated funds. Likewise, savvy donors are suspicious of telephone fundraisers, either because of security concerns about not sharing credit card information over the phone, or because they know the costs will be deducted from donations.

On the other hand, social media feels more real and personal. Although there may be paid staff creating and posting the stories, pictures, and videos on Facebook, Twitter, and YouTube, the costs aren't as glaring as with direct mail and telemarketing. More importantly, social media creates a level of engagement and connection that can't be duplicated offline. And whereas older donors may still be receptive to mail and phone, a younger generation is likely to be less so.

People in their 20s and 30s may not be making major financial gifts, but socially conscious young adults are ideal volunteers, and organizations that get them in the habit of giving now are likely to create a life-long donor relationship. Overwhelmingly, this demographic doesn't use landline phones (making them more difficult to reach by telemarketers) and prefer e-mail to postal mail. But they *are* on social media daily, and what they see and what friends recommend influences behavior.

Social media is also an effective way to reach the over-40 demographic, as more and more adults engage online at all ages. Recognize that a growing majority of all but the very youngest and very oldest people are active on one or more social media platform, providing you with new opportunities to connect and engage.

Whether you're a long-established organization or a new, small group, branding should be a major part of your social media presence. Young adults may not automatically recognize your organization's name and mission, even if it has been around for a century. Or they may have a vague— and outdated or incorrect—notion of what you do that falls far short of your current mission, leading to missed opportunities for support. Older potential donors and volunteers may be stuck in the past when it comes to thinking of your organization, not realizing that your mission and scope of services may have broadened or shifted dramatically with time. People who don't know what you do can't be passionate about your cause, and without passion, it's much more difficult to engage people as donors, supporters, and volunteers.

Credibility is another issue to address for today's audiences, who have become wary with online scams and news stories recounting the actions of unscrupulous charities. Expect potential donors and volunteers to check you out on sites like Charity Navigator with an eye toward how funds are used. Savvy donors know to ask how much of the funds raised actually go to client services (as opposed to marketing and administrative costs), another reason why slick direct mail or telemarketing can raise a red flag.

Your outreach on social media needs to tell a compelling story about the need and your organization's response. To engage potential donors, volunteers, and supporters, you need to awaken a passion to solve a problem. You'll also need to engage the heart (action, passion) as well as the head (credibility, awareness). Fortunately, social media's multi-media capability makes it easier than ever to use photos, videos, audio, and short vignettes to capture attention, educate, and make an emotional connection.

Social media also enables cause-centric organizations to expand their influence through the viral nature of online content. Unlike direct mail, social media enables your target audience to share content they find meaningful, so you gain access to each person's fans, friends, and followers. That can increase your reach exponentially, with the additional benefit that forwarded and shared content carries extra credibility because it is being passed on by a trusted source, a personal connection.

Now that you know how social media can extend your organization's reach and deepen its relationship with donors and volunteers, let's look at ways to use individual platforms.

LinkedIn, Facebook, and Twitter

Use LinkedIn for the business side of charity. Stay connected with your board members, donors, corporate sponsors, and volunteers, and realize that when you engage them about your organization, you are also engaging their personal networks of contacts as well. Craft your outcome stories with an eye toward enticing corporate sponsors and encouraging corporate volunteerism. Use photos, videos, and short text stories to make your mission and results real. Share metrics, and talk about how your work not only benefits the recipients of your services, but also the community as a whole. Realize that although the business audience on LinkedIn may appreciate heartwarming stories, posts that emphasize return on investment for time and donations are likely to be more effective in wooing new partners and keeping existing partners engaged.

LinkedIn is also a great place to thank your corporate sponsors, donors, and volunteers. You can't thank people enough in a public forum. Use photos and video to make it personal. Thank organizations and individuals. Every thank-you post not only builds goodwill, but it also showcases the "who's who" that is involved with your organization, which may prompt others in their circle to want to join the action. Creating share-worthy posts means your corporate colleagues are promoting your organization to their circles of influence, which is a form of endorsement.

Do a little detective work on LinkedIn and see who your donors, sponsors, and volunteers are connected to. Doing so makes it very easy to ask for a warm introduction, either in person or online, to others who are likely to be demographically perfect for your organization. Identify a wish list of people you'd like to approach and who might be best to ask. Be on the lookout for "superstars"—high profile or high net worth individuals and/or celebrities who are connected to your sponsors, donors, and volunteers. Leveraging a personal connection to someone with a massive public platform can create huge PR benefits for your organization. Celebrities are overwhelmed with requests from strangers, but may be very open to getting involved with your organization if asked by a family friend, old college roommate, or cousin.

When you're in the midst of responding to a crisis, don't forget to post urgent needs for cash, goods, services, volunteers, in-kind donations, trucks, equipment, specialized skills, etc. on LinkedIn. The business audience on this site can make things happen with a phone call, and may be very willing to step in to help on a local, regional, or national/international level. Resources that seem huge to your organization may be a minimal expense (and a deductible one at that) for a large organization. I witnessed first-hand the lengths that a large department store chain went to after Hurricane Katrina and Hurricane Rita to locate their displaced employees and help out with privately marshalled truckloads of essential food and supplies that got into stricken areas faster than most other aid organizations. Combine the desire to be a good corporate citizen with personal or organizational ties to a region in addition to the benefits of positive PR and you may find that your LinkedIn connections can move mountains in an emergency.

Facebook and Twitter connect you to the general public, including noncorporate volunteers. Both sites can be powerful in helping you tell your story to a large number of people with the use of compelling videos, photos, and short-but-heartfelt text. Although outcomes and results still matter, the people you'll reach on these sites will respond to emotion and stories about the impact on individuals, families, and communities. The warm and fuzzy approach counts for a lot in winning hearts and getting likes or shares. Tug at the heartstrings in appeals for help or stories about happy endings facilitated by your organization.

Stories are the source of your social media success. They're effective when you share them, but they are even more so when they're captured on video featuring the real people whose lives are better because of what your organization does, and the volunteers who help make that happen. Encourage your clients and volunteers to share their experiences, and reward them by thanking them and sharing their content. Do casual interviews and profiles of your volunteers and the community organizers who help bring people together. When they post and share them, you reach their friends and followers with the power of a personal endorsement.

Use Facebook and Twitter to share in-the-moment urgent needs that can be met by regular people—canned food, winter coats, bottled water, supplies for disaster areas, homes for shelter pets, and the need for emergency helpers with special skills such as doctors, nurses, EMTs, utility workers, construction professionals, truck drivers, and so on. When individuals rally their friends, family, and community to the cause, encourage them to document with photos and videos—a situation where selfies are awesome! Thank them publicly and profusely, utilizing photos and videos as well as text.

VIDEO RULES THE ONLINE WORLD

Facebook Live, Periscope, and Snapchat can help you and your volunteers show the devastation from a disaster, go live at a food drive, fundraiser, or resource collection point, bring viewers the real-time experience of building a Habitat for Humanity house, filling grocery bags for a food bank, or other project. (Always respect the privacy of your recipients and never show faces or give names without permission and a signed release form.) The objective is to bring your social media audience into the situation, sharing the urgency or encouraging them to get involved.

Most cause-centric organizations spend a lot of effort educating people about their mission and the need for their services. Social media makes it easier than ever to share photos, video, stories, and testimonials in a compelling way to awaken urgency and spur action. You can also share photo memes and short tweets and posts on tips or facts related to your cause, promote a hotline, or share links where people can access resources. Not only can you reach a wide audience with your information, but you can also track engagement through the likes, comments, shares, views, and retweets. A short video is particularly good for communicating essential tidbits and attracting maximum social media attention.

When you hold fundraisers, set up a "red carpet" photo spot with a backdrop of your logo, like you see at the Academy Awards or Comic Con, and encourage your donors to take and post selfies in front of the backdrop. People like to be caught doing something good.

Don't wait for the media to discover your fundraisers, community projects, relief projects, and urgent needs. Tag bloggers and local, regional, and national media on your tweets and posts. Upload video from disaster sites and relief efforts to sites like CNN and *Huffington Post*. Cultivate social media connections with sympathetic reporters and bloggers, and become their source for information pertaining to your organization's cause. Here's a place where everything I've talked about concerning branding, credibility, and influence comes together. Reporters will be more willing to tap you as a subject matter expert on your cause if they recognize and trust your brand, if your organization has a record for credibility and good behavior, and if you are visibly connected (and, therefore, informally endorsed) by other influential people the reporter trusts.

MONITOR YOUR BRAND

Guard your organization's reputation to maintain your credibility. One great way to do that is to use social media to listen. Several years ago, one international charity went through a scandal that disillusioned many donors and supporters. Even though the organization had a lengthy history and well-known brand, its credibility took a big hit. Instead of stonewalling, going defensive, or mounting a feel-good PR counteroffensive, the organization went on social media and asked people to talk to them about the crisis. They purposefully engaged in an online conversation that was sometimes uncomfortable, answering with transparency and honesty. It was a first step in restoring the organization's trustworthiness. Though it's best not to ever need to do damage control, when the worst happens, realize that social media can be the place to begin to rebuild trust.

Use tools such as Google Alerts to assure that you see when your organization's name is mentioned online. Hire someone to set up a Wikipedia page about your organization, and check the page periodically to make sure crowdsourced information doesn't introduce incorrect information. Google your organization regularly to see what comes up in the results. Go deeper with tools such as IceRocket, SocialMention, and Topsy to dig into how your company is showing up on Facebook and Twitter. Consider an inexpensive reputation management program such as Reputology to help you gather information easily.

Although it would be nice if everyone agreed on social causes, the reality is that cause-centric organizations often have vocal opposition, and may face hostile comments or even detractors who post false information. If your organization has a controversial focus, proactive and consistent reputation management is a necessity. You do not want negative comments or misinformation to gain momentum and become difficult or impossible to rebut or correct. Though dealing with an online crisis is uncomfortable, the potential for disaster from doing nothing is far worse.

Social Validation

Social validation happens when people follow what other, more influential people are doing and do likewise. It's the principle behind celebrity endorsements and high-profile product placements, and it's alive and well online—and easier than ever for you to harness for your organization.

We're used to thinking of social validation in terms of highly influential people—politicians, athletes, TV and movie stars, and other "famous" people. There's certainly still value in tapping the traditional forms of validation, such as high-profile speakers at an event, or having a well-known celebrity as a spokesperson. Yet today's online generation is more skeptical, realizing that most "spokespeople" are really paid endorsers.

Live events have limited attendance, and traditional media such as newspapers, magazines, and TV are waning in their influence.

Social media can provide social validation when an influential person with a large online following generates or retweets favorable content about your organization. Here's where it pays to know about connections your senior management, board members, loyal donors, and clients may have with famous or highly visible people. Asking someone to tweet or retweet requires much less time, effort, and commitment than recruiting them as a spokesperson, but one tweet from a celebrity can reach millions of people from a source they deem credible and worthy of emulation.

Although your radar should always be on the lookout for big fish, don't overlook the cumulative power of highly connected but not-famous people. Many bloggers, podcasters, subject matter experts, and gregarious individuals have built large online followings on the basis of their personality, perspective, and valuable information. They have high credibility with their online followers, and can have a reach in the tens of thousands or more. That individual following might not match that of a single Hollywood actor or actress, but when grouped together with similarly well-connected online personalities, the numbers quickly add up.

Another benefit of targeting "nearly famous" influencers is the ease of access. Getting to a major celebrity often involves going through layers of gatekeepers (unless your board member happens to be a close personal friend or family member), and can involve lengthy negotiations. By comparison, reaching out to "famous enough" influencers is as easy as sending an e-mail or a direct Twitter message. You'll spend some time identifying likely partners and compiling contact information, but your interactions will be direct, not filtered through agents and go-betweens.

Before contacting any influencer, ask yourself what's in it for them, and why they would want to agree. Social validation is most effective when the influencer has a personal, sincere connection to the cause. It can backfire spectacularly if the public suspects that any kinds of quid pro quo considerations have been made that aren't explicitly made known.

Take time to read the blogs and social media feeds of the influencers you think might be a good fit. Ideally, the person should be known and well-regarded by the audience you want to reach. This is where demographics come into play. If you're trying to reach young adults, the celebrities and online personalities with the most influence may be completely unfamiliar to your board members.

Look for natural connections. Does the person you're researching already have an affinity for your type of cause? Are they already talking about issues in your realm? Pay attention to more than just their content. Is the social persona of the individual something that would favorably represent your organization? An influential person with an interest in your cause might still do more harm than good if they are combative online or if the rest of their content is at odds with your organization's brand.

Resist the temptation to just tag famous people and hope they'll respond. That is viewed very negatively and likely to result in complaints to the social media site and/or a backlash. Influencers are highly protective of their credibility and following, with good reason. They will not appreciate being tagged in posts that run counter to their opinions, so do not presume or suggest endorsement without their permission.

When is it appropriate to tag someone on Facebook or Twitter in relation to your organization? If the person is attending your public event, serving as a spokesperson, or involved with your organization in a public way, tagging is okay and desirable. If you're retweeting them, quoting them, or referring to their work or to an article, media interview, and blog post featuring them that somehow relates to your mission, then tagging is perfectly fine. If they begin to engage with your organization by retweeting, liking, and commenting on your organization's posts and a relationship develops, then tagging them on important content occasionally (don't abuse the privilege) may get a high-profile retweet. Just go slowly, feel your way, and don't wear out your welcome.

CAUSE-CENTRIC CROWDFUNDING AND PEER-TO-PEER CAMPAIGNS

Social media has proven extremely effective for fundraising, especially from young adults. Being able to respond to a request for targeted donations on a mobile phone with the click of a button appeals to donors who are at home in an online world. Not only is giving via social media easy and immediate, but it lends itself to going viral with a little gamification.

Big donors have often been public about their philanthropy, either for social recognition or to inspire others to follow their example. New peer-to-peer fundraising software combines the reach of social media and the challenge of gamification to enable ordinary people to make a public declaration of their support for a favorite cause or organization and encourage their friends to join them—or even compete to hit goals. This is so much more than posting "please support this cause." Peer-to-peer fundraising empowers individuals to make a difference in the world for a cause that fires their passion.

If you're an organization person and the idea of turning individuals loose to fundraise gives you the willies, realize that peer-to-peer campaigns are nothing new. They are behind every charity walk-a-thon and 5K challenge, every kid selling wrapping paper or fruitcake, and every college student collecting spare change from motorists or dancing for 24 straight hours. From that perspective, these new online sites provide far more accountability and tracking than putting a jar on the counter of the local coffee shop. Even more importantly, peer-to-peer social media fundraising campaigns are easy to share with an individual's worldwide network of friends and colleagues, and they create social value out of good-natured one-upmanship.

Charitweet enables people to donate as little as one dollar directly to the charity of their choice—and challenge their social media followers to match their donation. Charitweet only works with cause-centric organizations vetted through CharityNavigator, and emphasizes transparency.

Classy is a mobile app/social media tool for peer-to-peer fundraising and crowdfunding, including event registration capabilities. It grew out of its founders' experiences organizing a pub crawl for charity, and seeks to make it easy for people to rally their friends to raise money for causes about which they are passionate. Classy can also be used by cause-centric organizations to hold ticketed or online fundraising events with their template pages, making it easy to get up and running without proprietary programming on your own Web page.

Similar sites include FirstGiving and CrowdRise. All of these social media tools are second-generation improvements similar to GoFundMe, with slicker interfaces, better mobile apps, and more built-in resources. CrowdRise is primarily for peer-to-peer campaigns, but can be used by organizations as well. FirstGiving also supports organization-drive campaigns and peer-to-peer. If you're looking for an enterprise scale, cloud-based solution, check out Blackbaud, which offers a suite of products to run all of your online fundraising along with templates to make it easy.

All of these sites offer a wealth of free resources to help organizations and individuals make their fundraising efforts more effectively.

Peer-to-peer fundraising enables individuals to make a statement about causes they care about, and use social media to make a personal "ask" (which anyone familiar with donors knows is the most effective way to raise money). Social media fundraising rewards people for doing the right thing, something traditional campaigns do for big donors, but which is rarely done for small and micro donors. By going public with their peer campaigns, individuals gain a sense of ownership over the results, and an emotional investment in the mission of the organization.

Social media can be a powerful tool for cause-centric organizations, enabling you to increase your reach to donors, sponsors, supporters, volunteers, community leaders, and clients. Take advantage of what LinkedIn, Facebook, Twitter, and other sites can do to help you cement your brand, extend your influence, and reinforce your credibility.

THE LAST WORD

Tap into the power of social media to extend your connection with volunteers, donors, and community leaders. By leveraging social validation, gamification, peer-to-peer fundraising, and crowdfunding, as well as the power of in-the-moment photos and videos, your organization and its mission can become more compelling than ever.

NEXT STEPS

1. Connect with your executives, donors, key volunteers, and supportive community leaders on LinkedIn. Make a list of who is connected to big fish with whom the organization should connect. Strategize on the best way to ask them.

2. Investigate crowdfunding and peer-to-peer options and see what works best for your organization.

3. Review how your organization is already using social media. Come up with a site-specific/audience-tailored strategy that utilizes storytelling, results, photos, and videos to create compelling, sharable content.

INTERVIEW WITH CHARMAINE HAMMOND

Charmaine Hammond is a professional speaker and best-selling author with Hammond International Inc., Team Toby, and the Million Acts of Kindness Tour.

Q: What have you learned about social media effectiveness for cause-centric organizations?

A: Social media was a critical component of our Million Acts of Kindness Tour. We drove from Vancouver to Toronto and then to Michigan and the West Coast back to Vancouver, 10,000 miles over six weeks. We used LinkedIn to attract and connect with prospects and sponsors. It's a powerhouse social media platform. Decision-makers for corporate sponsorship aren't doing business relationship building and networking on Facebook and Instagram. They are on LinkedIn. Offline, it is a challenge to connect with the right person, the decision-maker, and ultimately get past the gatekeepers. But LinkedIn reduced my time building relationships by at least 60 percent because I could get directly to the right person.

We received an exceptional amount of attention from traditional media on our tour—radio, print, and TV. Social media allowed us to further the reach of our traditional media. For example, following a TV interview, we would preschedule 30–50 tweets about the interview (with the link) on TV or radio over the next 60–90 days. We also requested our champions and colleagues to retweet the clips and links. Social media helped broaden my reach and influence, strengthen the tour's credibility (especially when you have well-known people retweeting you), and make a difference.

I used Periscope a lot during our tour. One day when I was out walking our dog Toby and picking up dog poop in the dog park, I talked on Periscope about how workplace messes often get left and are not attended to, and we have to clean them up just like the poop in the park. I was amazed at the degree of interaction this video created. I discovered that people like seeing a little slice of life and then having it relate to a bigger topic of life or business—drawing comparisons. We got feedback from our poop bag sponsor that they loved the videos and the degree of engagement these live streams created.

I asked people to take pictures of us or themselves at our tour events and to live tweet or Facebook post them. They appreciated when I suggested which hashtags to use. Within three minutes, tweets were going live at our events to audiences we would not normally reach.

Using HootSuite to preschedule posts on Facebook worked very well because we knew that every day we would have photos and videos circulating that also supported our sponsors and the charities involved in the campaign. This helped us remain consistent while we were traveling, and was especially helpful when we had periods of time where we had no Internet access to post live. We also ensured that we regularly posted live tweets and posts whenever we could.

I learned that some social media platforms didn't work for me. The take-away was that when you're supporting other community organizations, pick social media platforms you really like to use, and are skilled at using. It is better to be highly effective with two or three platforms than to be on many and have infrequent posts or not feel comfortable with the platform.

We chose to use Facebook—my personal page, my professional page, Toby's page, YouTube, Instagram, LinkedIn, and Twitter to build a bigger following and share our message. We tried to be thoughtful about not overlapping audiences so as not to fatigue our followers. We staggered the posts and content from platform to platform so that we did not overwhelm people with too many posts at once or too much repetition.

Instagram was great for sharing graphics and hashtags, tagging sponsors, and using location tags. We wanted to create a sense of tribe on Facebook and Twitter. I could share content easily from my cell phone on those sites as well as Instagram and Periscope. Now we have added Facebook Live to the platforms we regularly use.

I learned the value of pictures, video, and of doing Facebook polls to get people engaged. The real issue is to get people engaged enough to share your content. We learned to improve how we encouraged audiences (at our events and speaking engagements) to share during presentations. At one event, I announced a challenge for everyone to do three live posts during the event and that we would pick a winner. People were excited to take on the challenge—more so, they were happy to help! We had to ask and remind them throughout the presentation and get them to use the hashtag and our Twitter handle. We put the hashtag and our handle on the nametags, slides, banners, and signs.

Q: What did you discover about social media's value with sponsors?

A: Social media was a significant priority for our sponsors and partners—both nonprofit and for-profit. The sponsors appreciated having access to our audience and they get to engage with my followers. We took a lot of photos and videos in front of the Fraserway RV–sponsored motor home with the big logos of our sponsors along the side of the RV. In fact, we made the RV our photo and interview backdrop. We were careful and selective about the photos and videos done in front of the RV, because we wanted to represent the sponsor(s) and their brands well.

Posting and tagging is informal endorsement. Commenting and sharing on sponsor pages for programs that weren't part of our tour also helped to share who they are and what they do. We tagged high-level influencers and media on positive posts about sponsors and charities on topics relevant to our message, our sponsors' message, and the tour to increase visibility for our sponsors.

Realize that sponsors use LinkedIn to check you out. Many entrepreneurs have poor or incomplete LinkedIn profiles and it will be important for them to devote time and energy to strengthening their profile, as many people go to LinkedIn before they go to your Websites.

We approached local businesses during the tour at every tour stop—banks, vets, stores, salons, etc. We told them about our local pet rescue charities and asked them to sell cut-out paw prints—we called it Toonies for Toby (the paw prints costs $2 CAD, a coin called a "toonie") and they posted the paw prints on their walls, then took photos of the walls and all the paw prints. We built goodwill with local businesses and charities. We posted the amount of money earned and gave 100 percent of those donations to the charities, then shared that news with pictures on social media.

Because there were so many different types and levels of sponsors—the wrap for the RV, gift cards, poop bags, cash sponsors, technology partners, dog treats, etc.—messaging was very diverse. We tried to keep it from feeling fragmented—kept it anchored on the core message of a million acts of kindness— and we used our tagline in memes and on posts to help with consistency.

Social media has provided nonprofits with a whole new way to communicate their story and demonstrate the impact of what they do and who they serve. Whether it be video, photos (for example, at events and fundraisers), or live streams, social media allows nonprofits to build relationships and share their stories.

Social media allows nonprofits to thank sponsors and donors, show donors/sponsors and their following how the support/ funding has been utilized. This was very powerful.

Nonprofits use social media to promote events (for example, Facebook event pages), and build a strong following. They can also tag media, which is a way of getting notifications to media in an immediate way.

Social media has huge benefits to the nonprofits who have learned to use it correctly (for example, doing memes with tips and resources).

INTERVIEW WITH SHAWNE DUPERON, PhD

Q: What did you learn about social media's impact on cause-centric organizations in your work with *Project Forgive*?

A: The best way to get people involved is to share your stories. Most nonprofits post pictures of their volunteers. Share stories. Tell people what problems you solve. What do you inspire people to do? Share 60-second videos (or shorter). Touch people's hearts. People give to organizations that touch their hearts.

We did 40-second clips from our documentary. The documentary is free. We told people, if this inspires you, please donate.

The biggest change is that with social media, nonprofits can be more impactful than ever before.

The escalation of the use of video is mindboggling. They might soon be the biggest thing on Facebook. Always use subtitles, so people can get your message even if they have the sound turned off.

Twitter lets you share video. And of course there's YouTube. YouTube is powerful because of its user base, but also because it is a true search engine so your content is more findable. LinkedIn is searchable too. Facebook is not a search engine. It changes the algorithm frequently, and punishes you for having a successful strategy. YouTube doesn't seem to be doing that. Tumblr is good for reaching the 18–24 age group, and so is Snapchat. It all depends on your demographic. Stay where you are seeing success.

A benefit for nonprofits of using LinkedIn is that they'll find philanthropists and corporate sponsors on LinkedIn that they won't find on Facebook.

Twitter is really gossip influence. It works well when an organization needs to raise money to deal with a catastrophe. Use trending hashtags. But you've got to build trust before you ask for money.

Try stuff. Experiment. You could set a new trend. Facebook Live is becoming essential. The analytics go way up when people watch video, and you can take those metrics to sponsors to convince them to underwrite you. When you use video, use one person on camera talking directly to the viewer; it's very intimate. We've found that when it looks like a TV news interview, it's not as successful because people mistrust the media and institutions.

CHAPTER SEVENTEEN

TIME IN A BOTTLE: CAPTURING HISTORY ON SOCIAL MEDIA

Social media has democratized the collection, curation, and sharing of our history. Photos, documents, audio, and video can be archived and accessed easier than ever before, along with the words and voices of participants and observers. It's changing how we remember who we were and understand how history makes us who we are.

History takes many forms. Individuals dig into genealogy to discover their family story. Local historians try to preserve locations, photographs, documents, and accounts of events to maintain a complete record of a town's past, to cement a sense of place. Professional historians with museums and universities not only look to preserve history—for a subject, locale, or nation—but also to make sense of the fragments of the past, to view what has come before with new eyes and a fresh perspective.

One of the hardest jobs for historians has always been documentation. During much of history, a large part of the population was illiterate, so written records were relatively scarce. Those that were created owed their existence to the powerful and privileged, made by and for the Church, kings, or wealthy patrons who more often than not, had an agenda or at least a version of events they wanted to promote.

As literacy spread, more people wrote letters or kept journals and diaries, but once again, this was largely the purview of the middle and upper classes, and paper is fragile. Newspapers and magazines retained archives, but whole segments of the population (women, minorities, lower-income people, LGBTQ individuals, recent immigrants, teenagers) went largely or completely absent in their coverage. Archives burned or were lost to floods, and records vanished due to neglect. Letters to the editor revealed a small sampling of common opinion, but even those were filtered by editorial choice. The day-to-day thoughts of the average person were ephemeral, voiced at the dinner table to family or at the local pub to friends. Only the loudest voices remained preserved by the public record.

Historians do the best they can with such a spotty and incomplete record, but large gaps remain. Now, the Internet has begun to change how professional and amateur historians and genealogists do their work, as digitization and social media radically change how we preserve, access, and share content.

THE WRITTEN RECORD

Because the historical documents that did survive were fragile, access was usually limited in order to preserve paper from exposure to light, air, and handling. At best, this required physically traveling to a library, university, museum, or court house and negotiating access to a rare book room, periodicals archive, or special collection. Hours and availability were limited, and sometimes permission was difficult to obtain.

Just discovering the existence of written documents could take years of painstaking detective work. Many letters and journals in private collections were open only to scholars. Other journals or private correspondence remained in the hands of family and were not known or available at all. Because the storage of the physical documents was fragmented, indexing was either nonexistent or occurred through the notes of one researcher passed on to colleagues. Cross-referencing could only be done manually.

Documentation about the personal lives of the working class or individuals in marginalized groups was spotty at best. Edward S. Curtis and Rodman Wanamaker photographed Native American tribes at the turn of the 20th century, but although their photographs preserved some aspects of the lifestyle and culture, it was not a record created, compiled, or curated by the individuals themselves. That was true of similar efforts, like Doris Ulmann's Appalachian photography, or the photos of freed former slaves by the Federal Writers' Project and the Freedman's Bureau. Ethnographers might collect oral histories, and sometimes, writers like Studs Terkel made the real-life stories of working people into best-sellers, but the records were far from comprehensive, documented by outsiders, and subject to interpretive bias. The ability to document anything depended on the interest of organizations or wealthy individuals and the availability of funding. The information collected, because it was compiled and collected by outsiders, remained vulnerable to omission and subjectivity, and those who were interviewed or photographed had no control over their images or the final form of their stories, creating some incentive to shade the facts.

Social media's effect of chronicling life in real-time is giving historians a new perspective on recent and contemporary history. In the past, people often did not value contemporary resources because they were current, and therefore not thought of as "history" until time passed. Unfortunately, by the time the information was deemed important, it was often also more difficult to validate; eyewitnesses had died or memories dimmed, and documents had been lost or destroyed as unimportant.

Researchers are learning to compile information as it unfolds, instead of the more traditional perspective of looking back. Social media also enables projects like The Southern Food Ways Alliance of the University of Mississippi, in which scholars and writers all over the world are using the study of food to understand Southern society, race, gender, and immigration history. The project relies on the digital connectivity of scholars and writers, as well as on Facebook posts of what people eat.

Fragmented documentation posed particular difficulties for genealogists. Family members might share photocopies of important photos and documents, but filed away in a drawer, they remained largely inaccessible. If distant cousins researching within the same family did not know each other, few avenues existed to discover each other's projects and share information. Computer bulletin boards, listservs, e-mail lists, and online chat rooms began to pick up some of the slack as amateur researchers looked for ways to find one another. Breakthroughs came by word of mouth, or by sheer luck to stumble upon either a new resource or knowledgeable researcher.

Libraries, museums, large private collections, and universities began the shift to preserve documents and more easily share them years ago by scanning periodicals to microfiche. Film was less fragile than paper, but the process was slow and manual, and reading the film required long hours in the library basement hunched over a special piece of equipment.

With the Internet came digitization and a sudden explosion of documents made available online. Maps, census information, Selective Service registration, ships' manifests, immigration documents, public records (such as birth, death, and marriage certificates), survey documents, cemetery plot maps, newspapers, magazines, letters, and journals now started to pop up online. Some of the material was digitized by government agencies, institutions or with grant money, some by volunteers, and others by dedicated individuals. Thanks to Google, the information could not only be found more easily, but contents could be searched and cross-referenced. As databases replaced paper record-keeping, that information also became more easily accessible, either via online searches or through services like Lexus/Nexus.

Once computers and scanners became cheaper, many more individuals could easily preserve and share private troves of information such as family letters, journals, and certificates. Small museums, libraries, and newspapers could get in on the act with the help of volunteers as the technology became affordable. Suddenly, massive amounts of information became accessible and searchable—for free—for anyone, anywhere. Gatekeepers no longer controlled access, unless someone needed to see the original document. Distance, office hours, and physical location no longer posed barriers. Amateur and professional researchers found themselves with an embarrassment of riches.

But although digitization coupled with the Internet radically changed the collection and sharing of written documents, it also altered the notion of curation. Without gatekeepers and official protectors, there was also no one to categorize or consolidate information, create indices, validate legitimacy/authenticity, or preserve long-term access. There's more information available than ever before, but you're on your own when it comes to putting the pieces together. Caveat emptor.

Social Media Changes Everything

Social media is the glue that pulls digitized history together. Through the Websites and Facebook pages of museums, libraries, universities, private collectors, genealogists, and historians, digitized documents are being shared, indexed, and contextualized. These pages make the information easier to search and to cross-reference. Moreover, e-mail and social media make it so much easier for conversations to happen, questions to be asked and answered, introductions to be made, and information to be shared.

Museums large and small began sharing digitized collections from their archives free online. I've dug deep into some of these amazing resources in writing my historical fiction novels, and it is astounding to find the maps, photographs, and old corporate information that is readily available. Larger libraries and government agencies also began to make more of their archives accessible for free via the Internet. Though it can still require some historical detective work to piece information together, the pieces are now much easier to find and it's easier to notice the gaps where missing information ought to be.

Facebook may seem an unlikely place to dig for history or genealogy, but check into the many Facebook groups dedicated to those topics as a starting point. Groups can be the perfect venue for meeting people with similar interests, finding out about difficult-to-discover resources, getting tips from more experienced researchers, and being able to ask questions. Because researching can become something of an obsession, you might also enjoy the companionship of others who share your passion and will be excited to hear about your latest "find."

Try typing in some keywords that describe the information you're looking for into the search bar on Facebook. You might be surprised at what turns up. I found a Facebook page dedicated to my small hometown that was run by someone from its historical association. Not only was the page fun because of the crowdsourced photos and information shared by current and former residents, but it became a fascinating and ongoing conversation as people tried to confirm half-remembered details or identify faces from long-ago pictures. I also gained a substantial amount of information that I later used when I wrote a novella set in that town in the late 1800s.

Digitized scholarly papers and dissertations offer additional resources, as does Google Books, making many out-of-print or difficult to find books searchable. Digitization coupled with the power of search engines make fragments of data findable that would have been missed by traditional researching methods.

Many organizations and scholarly groups involved in genealogy have active pages on Facebook. Google "genealogy on Facebook" and you're likely to find frequently updated lists of links to some of the new and established pages.

Most of the history and genealogy sites have some capability for social interaction, even if it's just an e-mail address to contact the administrator. The big genealogy sites are generally crowdsourced, just like Wikipedia, with interested individuals uploading information and adding details or corrections. As with any online community, if you show up frequently, provide helpful information, answer questions, and refer resources, you'll get to know the regulars, who may prove invaluable to your own search.

Sites like Ancestry.com and Genealogy.com have created a central repository for researchers to find and share digitized information. I can attest to the thrill of finding my grandfather's draft card from World War I with his signature on it. Connecting with the past suddenly became easier and far more searchable than ever.

FamilySearch.org is a huge collection of family information encompassing records for millions of people worldwide. Afrigeneas is a site specializing in African-American family history, whereas JewishGen traces Jewish genealogy. BillionGraves and FindAGrave make it easy to search cemetery records. The National Archives, Fold3.com, the General Land Office (GLORecords.blm.gov), and the USGenWebProject.org make it easy to access U.S. government records. NewspaperAchive.com provides an extensive compilation of digitized newspapers searchable in many ways. The Library of Congress (LOC.gov) is also an amazing resource. If you know the name of the cemetery where your relatives are buried, odds are increasingly good that the cemetery itself may have an online database of plot numbers and names, which is likely to include photos of tombstones and date of interment.

At a certain point, genealogy and general history become intertwined, because the story of many small towns and regions is often driven by the fortunes and misfortunes of its most famous and prosperous families. This is also the case with the history of large organizations that provided the majority of a city's or region's jobs or were the primary reason an area became settled.

Looking for a corporate "genealogy" utilizes many of the same resources I've mentioned, with a few extra. Start with Google, and try variations of the most recent as well as prior versions of the company name. Look for industry records that might have a cross-link. Some industries have dedicated historical organizations committed to preserving a record of the companies and their workers (for example, coal mining in Pennsylvania). These small organization sites can have a trove of unique photos gathered from their targeted audience, and there's often an administrator who is passionate about the topic only an e-mail away. Check out the "Business Resources" section at the Library of Congress Website as well.

Flikr and Pinterest have become repositories for historical photos, not just those compiled by individuals, but also from the Smithsonian, National Archives, and New York Public Library, to name a few of the major organizations sharing through these sites. You can also post a photo and ask if anyone else can identify the person, place, or thing pictured, and gather a tribe of like-minded followers. YouTube has a slew of how-to videos for budding genealogists.

If you're researching a common topic with other people, consider creating a Wikipedia entry so that everyone can add, update, and correct information in one central site. Give a few of the more active and committed people administrative privileges, and encourage everyone involved to post information and to fact-check what others post. Remind your group to use photos and videos as well as text. Try to capture stories from elders about every question you can imagine, including their childhoods, holiday celebrations, family members, religious ceremonies, farming and trades, recreation, food, and all aspects of life. Those memories are precious and impossible to regain when an older generation passes on.

Get involved with the social media aspects of these sites, but always keep either a digital or screen print record of what you and those in your group post. Sites can decide to stop providing social media services, simply go out of business, or be bought, and you don't want to lose everything you've compiled.

HISTORY IN THE MAKING

How many times have you watched a history documentary as experts made educated guesses about how people from long ago carried on their everyday lives, speculating about what they ate or how the man-in-the-street thought about affairs of the day?

Future historians need only be able to access blogs and Facebook data to get a fairly complete picture of the lives of regular people—at least those from areas with Internet access. Thanks to social media, nonfamous, nonwealthy people can describe their lives in minute detail, share photos of their food and clothing, and air their opinions of current events. It's an unprecedented crowdsourced collection of history-in-the-making, and a goldmine for future historians and current ethnographers.

Think about the community organizations, houses of worship, alumni groups, and professional clubs that you belong to and look for opportunities to chronicle history via social media. Have volunteers on hand at events to record old timers talking about how things were "back in the day" with Skype or even with a cell phone video. Encourage storytelling with text and photos on the group's Facebook page. Start collecting photographs and memorabilia. Photograph and digitize everything, and then upload them to a wiki. If you're planning a celebration for a major milestone, like a centennial, begin well before the date—it will take longer than you anticipate to gather everything you need.

As facial recognition software becomes more widespread and inexpensive, we may finally be able to cross-reference people in old photos, assuming someone posts a picture that identifies the individual. This could be especially useful for families posting old photos in a central wiki, or for local historical organizations, both of which would have a high likelihood that multiple pictures of the same individuals might be uploaded.

THE LAST WORD

As social media tools continue to expand, professional and amateur historians and genealogists will find new and better ways to collect, preserve, and share their data and present a more complete picture of who we are and who we used to be.

NEXT STEPS

1. Remember to use the social aspects of online historical and genealogy sites to build relationships with others who share your passion. Build a network of individuals who share knowledge and resources. Be helpful, answer questions, and demonstrate your credibility.

2. Contribute to the cause by digitizing your family photos, letters, and documents and sharing them online.

3. Tap into the online archives of local and regional museums to piece together personal or community narratives.

4. Check back with large museums for expansions in their online archives.

INTERVIEW WITH TOM HANCHETT, PhD

Dr. Tom Hanchett is a community historian in Charlotte, N.C. He served as staff historian for 16 years at Levine Museum where he curated award-winning permanent and temporary exhibitions including *Cotton Fields to Skyscrapers* and *COURAGE*.

Q: How has social media changed the work of historians?

A: There are two categories to historical work: finding out stuff and disseminating information.

It is a digital revolution. We are able to sit at our computers and find so much. Five years ago, you could not have found out any of that.

The revolution is in being able to pull up isolated bits from hundreds of newspapers over dozens of years, information that would have been lost without digitization.

On the one hand, it democratizes the kind of history you can do. It makes for a much richer history. It has also democratized who can do history. People interested in history can tell richer, more complete stories than they could before.

If you're interested in genealogy, you can find things you couldn't have found before without needing to be a professional genealogist.

The more granular, the more stories you have, the harder it is to find a common narrative—the old gatekeepers were story aggregators, and helped us build a shared story. Now we have competing universes of shared stories. It's hard for opinions to coalesce into some kind of shared truth.

Q: What has the impact of social media been on capturing and preserving history?

A: Online resources are incredibly powerful—things that have been hidden away, little-known collections popping up without you needing to know they even existed. As everything is digitized, it's easier to put together a more complete story.

UNC-Charlotte's Living Charlotte project has compiled information about the city from the 1940s–1970s, fairly recent history. Even trained historians haven't thought deeply about some issues from that period because it's too recent. The project is scanning items that wouldn't be attractive to archivists yet. Often, it takes two to three generations before "information" becomes "history" instead of just our personal experience.

The benefit of crowdsourcing history is that it helps to identify people in photographs, places, events, and fill in missing information. The downside is that false information catches on and is hard to kill, and the Internet spreads it faster and further.

The Internet is helping more people find history accessible.

It will be interesting to see how historians winnow the primary source material being created right now. It'll also be interesting to see the impact of the decline of the giant trees of the media forest like newspapers, and today's parallel and conflicting media narratives. In the 1900s, we had letters to the editor in newspapers, which was a sampling of public opinion. Now, we have Facebook posts.

The digital world makes it easier for anyone to explore history, and that's a good thing. We still need historians, though. Their training makes them better at finding bits and pieces. The really important value they add is the ability to link particulars to the broader context. Those connections are what make history matter to readers.

INTERVIEW WITH LOUISE TODD

Louise Todd is a family history researcher with *www.familyhistorysimplified.com*. She has been researching her own family history for more than 35 years and has been a volunteer family history consultant for more than 15 years at the local Family History Center where she lives.

Q: How has social media changed the work of genealogists?

A: The biggest change is that people don't have to drive to the courthouse and find the archives of the physical birth/death records. It no longer takes six weeks to get information from Salt Lake City's massive archives, the Family History Library. It used to require looking at the micro film and microfiche and physically going to find the records, then paying to have them shipped back and forth or copied.

The last 4–5 years, there have been six million records being digitized by the Family History Library. Now you can go online and look 24/7.

The Internet has speeded up research. More is being digitized every day. The challenge is getting enough people to help index the information because it's all done by volunteers. There are great sites like FamilySearch.org and Ancestry.com.

Genealogy is the second most popular reason people go on the Internet. Social media has created all kinds of communities and Facebook groups and pages where people share information and articles.

Asking the Facebook "hive mind" and getting crowdsourced information and resources can help a lot. Social media helps people connect with relatives who are far away and promote genealogical events. So many cemeteries are online now with photos and an index of burial plots. And most of the digitization is volunteer-driven.

I always caution people that their family tree information can be difficult to validate without birth, death, marriage, etc. records. Stories get handed down over time, and details can be wrong. Sourcing is essential for accurate genealogical records, but it's difficult if all you have to go on are names and birthdates. The number one challenge is validating what relatives tell you because memory can be wrong. Now, it's easy to ask questions, get answers, and find resources.

In Canada, the most recent online census data is from 1921. In the United States, it's from the 1940s. That's because of privacy restrictions. The government won't release the next census data (1931) until most of the adults have passed. World War II records won't be available in Canada for a while yet for that same reason.

Other good sites: FamilySearch.org is very good with Asian/Chinese ancestry. Rootsweb is a good place to post questions. Cyndi's List is a good place to find resources. Great Britain controlled India before 1900, so look at UK online resources for family members from areas that were once colonies, and ships' manifests. More records from the Philippines are coming online soon. People use family trees (found on Ancestry.com or Familysearch.org) to consolidate family histories from multiple relatives. FamilySearch Wiki is another free online resource.

Conclusion

Imagining the Future

Social media has brought people together in ways that were unimaginable just a decade or so ago, enabling us to forge or rekindle personal connections while presenting affordable possibilities to expand branding, credibility, and influence on a global level.

Many businesses—large and small—are still catching up with technology, looking for ways to leverage these new opportunities and develop strategies to harness social media's potential to achieve their marketing goals.

It's a safe bet that social media platforms will continue to innovate and evolve. The companies poised to make the most of those changes will be ones with flexible strategies that can adapt as tools and user behavior shifts. Five-year plans are meaningless in the face of disruptive technology that is far from technological maturity. If you want to make the most of social media, you're going to need to learn to go with the flow.

No one can predict the next social media breakthrough. Yet it's possible to make some educated guesses based on emerging trends and technology. These shifts may have negligible impact on the way some businesses use social media and present enormous opportunities for others. It will be up to you to watch for new platforms and capabilities and see the possibilities they offer.

MOBILE MATTERS

Consumers have been shifting their online consumption from desktop computers to mobile devices for a while—and that's likely to continue. Three converging factors contribute to this: the increased computing power and capabilities of smartphones, the decreasing expense of bandwidth, and the widening availability of Wi-Fi access.

Phones are now essentially small computers, and some of the larger versions blur the line between the phone and mini tablet. It's only natural for consumers to take advantage of that computing power on the go. Users may still access sites from both their computers and their phones, but they will expect the experience to be identical regardless of the device, and will demand performance to be device-agnostic. So if your Website isn't mobile compatible, you're at a serious disadvantage.

Can you offer a mobile app that makes it seamless and convenient for customers to access or use your service? Creating apps has gotten easier and less expensive. What kind of quick access to your services and information would benefit users? Whether it's getting a daily tip, inspirational message, or being able to order your product online, customers are likely to access your services more frequently if they don't have to log in each time or type in a URL to a browser.

VERTICAL INTEGRATION

We're already seeing major social media sites buying up compatible competitors or absorbing sites that offer complementary services. That consolidation is likely to continue as social media sites mature. When sites acquire other platforms, those capabilities get integrated into a seamless whole. We're likely to see more such vertical integration in the future, and that may lead to the silo-ing of sites that no longer play well with each other because of perceived competition, like what appears to be happening with Facebook and YouTube.

On one hand, vertical integration can make it easier to use compatible sites together, magnifying their reach and harnessing their unique strengths. On the other hand, if a tool you've relied upon is acquired by one "team" and other tools are acquired by a competitor, you may suddenly find yourself working around new complications. To use the Facebook/ YouTube example, people who have built up a large YouTube following and a significant amount of content on the site find themselves at a disadvantage if Facebook were to suppress links to YouTube in favor of "native" video or Facebook Live posts.

When this kind of shift occurs, you'll have to decide how to respond. Do you maintain content in both formats, shift your usage, or fine-tune each platform to reach different segments of your audience? Likewise, the platforms may rethink their tools and decide to repurpose them, as Google appears to be doing with Google Hangouts On Air. If you've built a following and a strategy around the capabilities of a single tool or site, be sure to have a backup plan. Many enthusiastic Blab users were stuck when the multi-user live video site abruptly shut down, taking their content with it. Never make any single site or platform the sole repository of your content. Back up or mirror everything of value.

The volatility of the social media landscape makes it all the more important for you to obtain e-mail addresses for your followers so that in the event that one of your platforms closes down a tool or just disappears, you can tell your audience where to find you and how to access your content. Your e-mail newsletter remains essential because it is a channel you control. (For even more security, export a copy of your mailing list to a spreadsheet and store it on your computer as a backup in case your e-mail platform was to suddenly change.)

VICARIOUS EXPERIENCE

Virtual reality, drone cameras, personal action cameras, smart glasses, and RFID (radio-frequency identification) tracking all suggest that as these technologies mature and align, we'll see social media evolve as a way to share our experiences in ways that go far beyond words, photos, and video clips.

We've had a taste of what location tracking can offer when apps suggest restaurants, hotels, discounts, and entertainment options based on where we're standing at the moment. Although some might find that to be intrusive, others will gladly trade off anonymity for convenience and bargains. Now imagine apps and social media sites that serve up a full travelogue of your experience for your followers with street-level video from an integrated action camera, smart glasses, or Periscope coupled with personal drone camera clips.

EXPERIENCE ENHANCEMENT

Smart companies will find ways to augment the social media experience as well as the in-person experience to create a personal documentary that is more than the sum of its parts. Just like Wi-Fi access has become a drawing card for hospitality businesses, we may find that this "meta" enhancement of the virtual/social media experience also becomes a differentiating feature, particularly with demographics with high technology and social media usage.

How can you make your customers' social media interactions more fun, satisfying, and individualized, and where does the opportunity arise to incorporate your branding? Offering cool digital enhancements that customers can incorporate into their social media stream can increase your visibility, cement your branding, and increase customer engagement.

How can you use social media to enhance your customers' experience with your services? Mobile apps that enable online buying, placing an order for take-out, or securing a reservation are already commonplace. A growing number of events have free apps that replace a bulky paper program and enable attendees to search for the performer, speaker, title, or topic they want. These apps also allow users to put together an individualized agenda so they don't have to keep flipping through the program, and make it easy for users to get the most out of the event by providing access to last-minute program changes, hours of operation, and so on.

How could you create a better, more customized, and more seamless experience for your customers using social media or a mobile app? Some industries will find more immediate opportunities than others, but any way you can reduce the friction of interfacing with your customer will score you satisfaction points. Or, to put it in another way, how can social media and mobile apps create a concierge-level of service for all of your customers?

THE LAST WORD

Social media is here to stay, and companies are absent at their own risk. If you're not engaging with your customers and prospects, your competitors probably are. Maximizing social media's possibilities goes far beyond merely posting updates. Think creatively about how you can use social media to revolutionize how your customers interact with you, solve their problems, and achieve their goals, and you'll be at the forefront of the digital revolution.

NEXT STEPS

1. As you integrate social media into your business and strategic plan, pay attention to new technologies, service enhancements, and sites that offer additional opportunities. The landscape is constantly changing.

2. What would "concierge-level" service encompass for your customers? How could you use social media to enhance their experience with your services and products? How might you anticipate their needs and exceed their expectations?

RESOURCES

COOL SITES YOU HAVEN'T HEARD OF

In addition to the many sites mentioned in the text, these are some other Websites and programs you may find useful.

www.1shoppingcart.com

www.AdMob.com

www.AdWords.Google.com

www.Alexa.com

Amazon Affiliate Program: *https://affiliate-program.amazon.com*

Amazon Author Page: *https://authorcentral.amazon.com*

http://audacity.sourceforge.net/

www.AudioAcrobat.com

www.AWeber.com

www.Biznessapps.com

www.BlogTalkRadio.com

www.Captcha.net/

www.ConstantContact.com

www.Delicious.com

www.Digg.com

www.Efax.com/

www.eSpeakers.com

http://eventful.com/

www.Evernote.com/

www.Flickr.com

www.Foursquare.com

www.FreeConference.com

www.FreeConferenceCalling.com

www.FreeConferencePro.com

www.Godaddy.com/

www.GoogleKeywordTool.com

www.GoToMeeting.com

www.Guru.com

www.LATalkRadio.com

www.Libsyn.com

www.Local.com

http://mailchimp.com/

www.PayPal.com

www.PodcastAlley.com

http://polldaddy.com/

www.PR.com

www.PRLeap.com

www.PRLog.org

www.PRNewswire.com

www.PRWeb.com

www.Quantcast.com

www.RadioGuestList.com

www.Shutterfly.com

www.Skype.com

www.Squareup.com

www.StumbleUpon.com

www.SurveyMonkey.com

www.TalkZone.com

www.TinyURL.com

www.VerticalResponse.com

www.Vistaprint.com

www.VoiceAmerica.com

www.WebSiteGrader.com

www.Wikispaces.com

http://explore.live.com/windows-live-movie-maker

INDEX

ABOUT THE AUTHOR

Gail Z. Martin is a best-selling author, international speaker, and new media marketing expert. She owns DreamSpinner Communications, a marketing consulting firm. Gail is the author of *30 Days to Social Media Success*, *30 Days to Online PR and Marketing Success*, and *30 Days to Virtual Productivity Success*. Gail holds an MBA in marketing and computer systems and has hit the best-seller charts on both sides of the Atlantic. *30 Days to Social Media Success* made TheWashingtonPost.com's Top 5 Business Books, was chosen by Fed-Ex Office and OfficeMax to be among a handful of books featured in-store, and has been mentioned in media including *Inc.*, *The Wall Street Journal*, *Worth*, and *Fox Business News*. *30 Days to Social Media Success* was named by LifeHack as one of the Top 20 Business Books to Read in 2016.

Gail's marketing and social media homepage can be found at *www.DreamSpinnerCommunications.com*. She tweets @GailMartinPR, is on Facebook as Gail Martin and 30 Day Results Guide, and blogs at *www.BigDreamsAndHardWork.com*,

On the fiction side of her world, Gail is the author of *The Shadowed Path* (Solaris Books); *Vendetta: A Deadly Curiosities Novel,* in her urban fantasy series set in Charleston, S.C. (Solaris Books); *Shadow and Flame,* the fourth and final book in the Ascendant Kingdoms Saga (Orbit Books); and *Iron and Blood,* a new steampunk series (Solaris Books), co-authored with Larry N. Martin. *Scourge: A Darkhurst Novel,* the first in a brand-new epic fantasy series, debuts from Solaris Books in 2017.

She is also the author of *Ice Forged, Reign of Ash,* and *War of Shadows* in The Ascendant Kingdoms Saga, The Chronicles of The Necromancer series (*The Summoner, The Blood King, Dark Haven, Dark Lady's Chosen*); The Fallen Kings Cycle (*The Sworn, The Dread*), and the urban fantasy novel, *Deadly Curiosities.* Gail writes three e-book series: *The Jonmarc Vahanian Adventures, The Deadly Curiosities Adventures,* and *The Blaine McFadden Adventures. The Storm and Fury Adventures,* steampunk stories set in the Iron and Blood world, are co-authored with Larry N. Martin. Her work has appeared in more than 35 U.S. and UK anthologies.

Find fiction details at *www.GailZMartin.com,* on Twitter @GailZMartin, on Facebook.com/WinterKingdoms, at DisquietingVisions.com (blog), on Goodreads at *www.goodreads.com/GailZMartin,* and with free excerpts on Wattpad at *http://wattpad.com/GailZMartin.*